JESUS HAS TWO DADDIES

TWO DADS, ONE FAMILY

By
Thomas McMillen-Oakley

Marshall - Michigan
800Publishing.com

Jesus Has Two Daddies: Two Dads, One Family

Copyright © 2012 by Thomas McMillen-Oakley

Cover design by Katie Horkey

Layout by Kait Lamphere

Author photo courtesy of author

The opinions expressed in this manuscript are solely the opinions of the author and do not represent the opinions or thoughts of the publisher. The author represents and warrants that s/he either owns or has the legal right to publish all material in this book.

ISBN-13: 978-1-938110-04-7

First published in 2012

10 9 8 7 6 5 4 3 2 1

Published by   2 MOON PRESS
                      123 W. Michigan Ave, Marshall, Michigan 49068
                      www.800publishing.com

All Rights Reserved. This book may not be reproduced, transmitted, or stored in whole or in part by any means, including graphic, electronic, or mechanical without the express written consent of the publisher except in the case of brief quotations embodied in critical articles and reviews.

PRINTED IN THE UNITED STATES OF AMERICA

This book is lovingly dedicated to the memory and legacy of Mrs. Virginia "Ginny" Huntoon.

AUTHOR'S NOTE:

Shortly after Anna's birth, I was asked to speak at the University of Michigan School of Social Work about our experience. I sat in a cramped classroom surrounded by eager grad students and a doting professor, and for two hours, I told our story to the assembled group. During a break, one of the students came forward and mentioned that our story needed to be told beyond this small group, and that what we went through to start a family was worth sharing with a larger audience. I agreed and mentioned that with a new baby, writing a book would be next to impossible. The professor jabbed her pen at my notebook, pointing to the outline of my talk. "There's your book!" she said. "An outline is by far the hardest part of any book. You just need to fill in the blanks now."

The outline sat on my desktop for several months, and when time allowed, I would add notes or stories that I felt were relevant to what we went through. I also began my blog at www.jesushas2daddies.com to share with our friends and families our daily lives with our new baby. What you have now is the culmination of six years of parenting and life with a precocious daughter and her boisterous brother. The *Field Observations* are those notes, stories, and moments that we felt added to the mix and help complete our tale of becoming a family. And, so you know who is who in the story, I am Papa and Tod is Daddy. I have also included a few sections titled *A Look Back* as these recollections help with the narrative as well.

After reading my manuscript for this book, my husband Tod felt that he needed to share his side of the story so that the reader would have a balanced view of what took place. The *Tod Chimes In* sections are there to complete the picture for you as you read our story. When we decided to become parents, there was a definite shortage of books on two dads intentionally starting a family. We want to share what life was like before and after kids for those out there that might be contemplating this adventure. Over the past six years, many of the blanks have been filled in, but our story is far from complete.

We welcome you to this adventure.

Sometimes I'm not good, sometimes I are.

~ A.L.M.O.

CHAPTER ONE:
GETTING TO KNOW US

IT IS SAID THAT there are two sides to every story, and I believe it. With that said, it was 16 years ago that Tod and I met. Many things were going on in our respective lives, but the stars aligned that night, and we've been together ever since.

I was hopped up on pain pills from my recent wisdom teeth extraction. Things were not well with my old boyfriend, and he was a little pissed that I chose to have my teeth pulled on his birthday. Frankly, I didn't care, I wanted a long weekend to recover and let the swelling go down (for the record, all four were yanked, with only nitrous and local anesthetic). The ex and his friends decided to go out and left me with the cat and the phone. I felt okay, the bleeding had stopped, and I was shocked that I didn't look like Marlon Brando. The phone rang, it was my friend Doug calling to invite me to a party. I thought it over, took some pain pills, and headed out the door. The night was a fog of faces and a dull thudding pain (kind of like the night Sarah Palin was nominated). One face stood out, and it's the face I wake up to each morning. People knew that I was still with the Latino-who-shall-not-be-named, so they were a little irritated that Tod and I left together that night. While it would have been fun to run off into the cover of night for some romantic escapade, it was pretty mild. We went back to his house and talked until late into the evening. Since it was Presidents' Day weekend, we both had Monday off and the Latino-who-shall-not-be-named had to work, so we spent the day in Ann Arbor, MI walking around, eating Korean food (note: not the best choice for your first solids after oral surgery), and watching *Mr. Holland's Opus* at the movie theatre. What else would you expect two teachers to go see on their day off?

*The perfect couple, K Fed and Britney.
And before you judge us, we won 1st place.*

As the weeks went on, we spent more time together, and I realized that it was over with the Latino-who-shall-not-be-named. After some discussion, Tod and I decided to start dating once I had officially called it off with the Latino-who-shall-not-be-named. Surprisingly, the talk with the ex went well; it was no big surprise for either of us. I moved my stuff out of the bedroom and took up refuge in the back bedroom. After "the talk," I went to Tod's, and we officially started dating.

Six months later, I moved in to Tod's house with my few possessions and a very pissed cat. The first couple of years together were not easy, they never are; it's called reality. But they helped us get ready for all the stuff that came our way with all the craziness associated with starting a family.

Tod Chimes In: *Isn't that a sweet story? Now let me tell you the real story about the first time we met. I had lived in Jackson for just over four years without meeting any other gay men my own age. On December 17, 1994 (two years prior to Tom's story) I went to Club Paradise in Lansing. Richard, an acquaintance I had made the week prior, introduced me to Tom knowing that we were both public school teachers and that Tom used to work at the camp where I took* *my sixth grade students. Tom talked to me for less than five minutes not to be seen again for another 14 months. When I reminded him of this when we met again in 1996, he told me about his jealous, Latin boyfriend, how my long hair scared him off, and a case of mistaken identity with another teacher that used to work for the same school district. Whatever.*

Chapter Two:
So What's in a Name?

I grew up knowing the entire life story of Annie Oakley, Ohio's own Little Miss Sure Shot. Not only because we shared the same last name but because my dad was born in her hometown of Greenville, Ohio. And, for the record, her real last name is Moses. In an ironic turn of events, Tod may actually be related to her on his grandpa's side of the family. Yes, Tod's grandpa is a Buckeye. This family secret came to light at his funeral when it was revealed that he was born in **gasp** Ohio.

When my teachers or complete strangers would find out my last name was Oakley, I would immediately be asked if I was related to Miss Sure Shot. After countless trips to the Garst Museum in Greenville and doing some of my own research for history projects, I could reply to these queries with a heavy sigh and an "it was only her stage name, Moses was her real name, but my dad was born in Greenville, Ohio, and they still have Annie Oakley Days down there. Did you want to know anything else?"

Usually this shut them up, and I could get on with whatever important adolescent project I was working on at the time. Now, people hear my last name and think of the sunglasses. If I had a nickel for every time someone asked me if I was related to the company, I might actually be able to afford a pair.

As Tod and I moved toward adoption, one question came to mind: how would we be represented as a family? We knew that Tod would adopt first since he had better insurance, but we didn't want to have two McMillens and an Oakley. So we talked to our lawyer and asked him about changing our last names in preparation for the child coming into our lives. We knew that if we had two different last names, there might be questions or problems as our child moved through school. We both have had students with a host of last names and parentage, so we wanted to minimize any confusion that our new family might bring.

Aside from the legal expenses, it's a pretty easy thing to do and according to our lawyer, common. For our anniversary, Tod's parents gave us a porcelain cross with McMillen-Oakley written under "Bless our House." We liked what we saw, so we moved forward with the name change. We had to get fingerprinted and swear that we weren't doing this to bow out of any debt or avoid any links to a criminal past before we could get our court date. Five years after we met in 1996, we had a commitment ceremony, a simple holy union performed by a local Unitarian Minister. In a typical wedding, the wife will often adopt the husband's last name. We didn't do anything with our last names in 2001, so this was our chance to legally join forces since actually being allowed to marry was still against the law in most of the United States.

Us on the day of our commitment ceremony in 2001.

Field Observation:
White Lies: Don't Do It (May 2009)

A recent poll on a Gay Parenting website asked if it was ever acceptable to lie to your children.

Oy.

This opened a massive discussion about what was ethical and what was not. Lies are okay. In fact, I encourage it. Kids are pretty much stupid and gullible.

Christmas and Santa? LIES!

Easter and the Easter Bunny? LIES!

The tooth fairy? More lies!

Parents have been lying for years, and it works. When you need a motivator to keep the kids in line behavior-wise, Santa or the Bunny can be that much needed carrot on the stick to keep the peace. This is one of the reasons why I love fall. It's the season of manipulation for both the parents and the kids. Every commercial Anna sees on TV is punctuated with an "I WANT THAT!" We fire back that she'll have to be good, Santa's watching, etc. She made the connection last year that Santa = gifts, so I think we're good to go, at least until someone at daycare or school spills the beans. I'm not worried about daycare as the daycare lady will have the child who blows the secret publicly flogged. At school however, we don't have as much control over what she hears.

However, there have been a few lies that I have put out to Anna that have backfired and caused more harm than good. Anna is good at opening car doors and windows and demands that her window be down while we are driving. This is both noisy and annoying, and she uses it to dump whatever she has in her hands out on to the street. So I decided to make it more in her interest to keep the windows up. I told her about the dreaded Freeway Monkeys. You can't always see them, but they're out there, and they'll jump in the car if you leave your windows down or doors unlocked. She accepted this without question, and her proclivity for unlocking the door and opening the windows stopped. However, she is now afraid of monkeys and needs to be dragged to see them at the zoo. A local car wash had a person dressed as a gorilla standing out front waving a sign. She saw the person and screamed "IT'S A FREEWAY MONKEY!" and began doing her fake sobbing in the back seat.

Nice.

Now her love of all mammals is tainted by this lie. However, she is now safe and won't be rolling out onto the pavement because she's messing around with the door. By the way, we do have the parental controls on, but she *insists* that she be able to control the doors and locks.

Lies aren't limited to parents. Grandparents can get in on it as well. For instance, we asked a set of grandparents (who shall remain unnamed) to watch the kids while we went off for a weekend of camping. Anna and Grandma headed out to buy school supplies and Grandpa stayed at home with Eli. Eli had a full diaper, and Grandpa had to call Grandma to come home to change it. When Anna talked to Grandpa about this, he said that he didn't know how to change poopy diapers and that only Grandma knew how to do it right. Good one Grandpa. We'll remember that.

I draw my line in the sand about what you can't lie about. Don't ever lie about how much you love your kids. Never say that you don't love them, instead talk about how you don't like their behavior. Separate them from what is bad and let them know that they are still loved. Love is precious, and it's something that you can never deny or use as a ploy for good behavior. However, from now until December 24th, Santa is your bitch, and you can use and abuse him all you want.

Chapter Three:
Our Day in Court

We headed to the courthouse on a cloudy, grey morning. We had to be in the judge's chamber at our cattle call time and had to sit through several other legal issues before our appointed time. Our lawyer dressed in his best suit and tie; we both opted for khakis and nice shirts. Going to court is usually a serious and important event as one is often there to represent themselves. From traffic issues to family problems, it's usually a sea of humanity flowing through the metal detectors into the courthouse.

Our house is at the southern end of the street where the courthouse is located, so we often drive by and witness the unwashed masses yearning for justice and a full set of teeth. The two places where you can't help feeling you are an extra from "Hee Haw" are the Secretary of State's Office and the county fair. Both are prime arenas for mullets and tube tops and a whole array of fashion and hygiene crimes. We're not here to judge these people, but I think if you're going to go before a judge, a NASCAR shirt or lime green sweatpants with "JUICY!" stitched on the ass are probably poor choices.

I didn't know what to expect. A name change is a common occurrence, but still an air of mystery and dread hung in the room.

What if the judge said no?

What if she figured out our secret homo-agenda?

What if... what if...

When I worked at a YMCA Camp right out of college, I was responsible for orienting the students that came to stay with us for the week. I would go through the rules and regulations and then would start the dreaded Q and A time. I prefaced the speech with the caveat that I would *not* entertain any "what if?" questions. As more often than not, these questions are usually looking for wiggle room and avoidance of any consequences. "So what if I sneak out of the cabin and TP the girls' cabin?" "So what if I accidentally fall in the lake?" Stuff like that. I should have taken my own advice and turned off the 'what if' generator in my mind and focused on what was in front of me that day. The thing that irritated me the most that day was that three marriages were dissolved in front of us in a matter of moments. The marriages often ended with only one party present. With the stroke of the judge's pen, whatever vows had been spoken were nullified. It pissed me off to sit and witness the ease in which these people separated. We were doing what we could to have the legal illusion of marriage and family at great expense, and these folks were dissolving their families before our eyes with the blessing of the courts.

When our time came, we each stood before the judge and explained to her (at the coaching of our lawyer) that this is how we were now known professionally (with the new name), and we were indeed crime free and not running from the law. We went one right after the other, and she didn't seem to blink as we did this. I secretly hoped that I would step up to the judge's area and be asked to swear to God on the Bible that I was telling the truth. I would refuse to do so and demand that Julia Child's *The Way to Cook* or a recent copy of *Martha Stewart Living* be brought forward for my swearing in. But that didn't happen. I don't remember being asked to swear that I was telling the truth or any of that *Law and Order* crime drama bullshit. A few million papers needed to be filled out at the clerk's office and then we were united legally by name. When we began the adoption process, we knew that we might have the chance to name our child, especially if we were matched with a newborn. We put together a spreadsheet of all of our family names and tech-wizard Tod began matching up names with names, both male and female, with the help of the program. We began with the female family names and our search quickly ended when Anna and Laura came up together in the cell. Anna is my maternal grandmother's name, and Laura is Tod's maternal grandmother's name. It seemed right that we honor our moms with this name seeing as we were honoring our fathers with the new combined last name. Don't get us wrong, we love our paternal grandmothers as well, but Bessie Martha doesn't exactly flow off the tongue.

If we were matched with a boy, we would have named him Dylan Robert. Tod's father is Robert, but we were going for Dylan Thomas, the Welsh writer and Robert Burns, the Bard of Scotland with the boy's name. None of the family names on the boy side were as lyrical as Anna Laura and some were downright weird. Mind you, we have names such as Grover, Marvin, Reo, and Lyle to work with, so we passed. On that muggy summer afternoon, the small but mighty Clan McMillen-Oakley had begun.

Field Observation:
A Turd in the Pool (July 2010)

I do all I can to keep my kids safe and sound on a daily basis. We live on a busy street, so since day one, I have pounded (gently) into the kids' heads that they can't play near the street. Once a year, we allow them to frolic in the street, and that's only when the annual Rose Parade makes its ponderous trek down our street toward the park for its finale. We have talked about stranger danger and all the other biggies, and we avoid places that might put them in danger on a regular basis (strip clubs, motorcycle gangs, ~~tattoo parlors,~~ etc.). Imagine my surprise when we go to a city pool to cool off and there is a guy there with an electronic tether on his leg.

OMG.

WTF?

Tod pointed him out first, and it wasn't long before Anna noticed it and asked what it was. I stammered for a minute and told her that it was a radio as I didn't want to scare her. I know that we need to live and let live in our world as that is what the good book teaches us. But there are some areas in life where I don't want to have to worry, and I want to be able to enjoy myself with my family. I don't know what this guy did, and I don't want to know. What bothers me is the fact that he was there while still under supervision by the Michigan Department of Corrections.

He might not be dangerous, but we don't know what he did to deserve this punishment, so the mind reels. There is a scene in Todd Field's 2006 movie *Little Children* that shows Jackie Earle Haley's character, a convicted sex offender (who is key to the plot), diving into a crowded public pool with a mask and snorkel. An observant parent recognizes him, sounds the alarm, and the pool is cleared quicker than when there is a shark warning on a beach. The camera catches him swimming around underwater, oblivious (or not) to the commotion he is causing on deck. That scene flashed in my mind as I watched this guy float around the pool taking pictures with his camera (why he was taking pictures, I don't know, it just added to the ick factor).

My heavily sun-blocked skin crawled in the staggering heat.

I posted this lovely tidbit of my life on Facebook and for the most part, the responses from my 400 + friends supported my WTF questioning of this guy being in a public space under police surveillance. There were however, some detractors who felt I wasn't giving him the benefit of the doubt and thought that I was being too harsh and judgmental. I stood firm though and pointed out that there are some places where criminals shouldn't go, including public pools with an emphasis on kids and toddlers. The rest of my short list would be petting zoos, the kids' area at any amusement park, the juvenile books department of any public library and any Toddlers and Tiara contests in the area.

My favorite quote from the Bible (the one that I like to toss around to all the fundies in my life) is Matthew 7, "Judge not, that you be not judged." But when it comes to my kids and their safety, I will judge you, and I will watch you, and you are guilty in my book until you are proven innocent, or you can prove to me that you are only doing time for check fraud.

Until then, watch your back and stay away from my kids.

Chapter Four:
Maslow and Me

When I was in college working toward my undergrad, I minored in Adolescent Psychology. I don't remember why, but it paid off when I began to teach at the high school level. As my students came in each year, I could see the various chapter headings from my psychology texts hanging over their heads as they took their seats. Little did I know that my classroom would be a perfect storm of adolescent angst and ennui each school year. This minor was worthless in the job market, but it did give me an edge in dealing with all they brought to the table in the classroom. It gave me the ability to see through my own bullshit on a regular basis as well. The theories I studied may have been aimed at working with kids, but they transcended time and age. So it was no surprise to me to watch as Tod and I grew as a couple and collectively chipped away at Maslow's hierarchy of needs.

While his pyramid has been scoffed at by some researchers, I think it hits home for most of us. At the base, the physiological needs are pretty obvious. If you don't do them, or have these, you die (with sex being the only possible exception). But then Maslow's work moves up to safety and security needs which include:

- Personal security
- Financial security
- Health and well-being
- Safety net against accidents/illness

When we went through our initial home study for the adoption, we had our entire life spread out on the dining room table for the social worker to review and approve. We had to prove that we could indeed offer our future child all these things by showing that we had jobs, life insurance, health insurance, and about 100 other things to demonstrate we would be worthy parents. I had to get up and walk around to control my growing frustration because I knew that as we met with our social worker, there were probably hundreds of couples, of all ages, from all around the world, having sex and unintentionally starting a family without the least bit of consideration to these issues. It didn't seem fair that we were put under the microscope, but these couples were procreating away with little regard for anything except the now.

It was perhaps the most frustrating and infuriating aspect of the whole adoption process. To quote Tod (no, not my Tod, rather, Keanu Reeve's character in the movie *Parenthood*):

"You know, Mrs. Buckman, you need a license to buy a dog, to drive a car–hell, you even need a license to catch a fish. But they'll let any butt-reaming asshole be a father."

Truer words have never been spoken.

I think back to all the students that I had at the high school where I taught and of all the potential that was lost because of unplanned pregnancies. One student, an aspiring artist, would share her travel stories with me each year and eagerly listen to my tales from New York and Chicago. She became pregnant her senior year, and her life and education went on hold. She returned a few years later for a visit with her child in tow, and we started talking about life. I asked her if she had done anything fun or checked out any art. She turned red and began crying as she described her situation at home. If they wanted to go and see a movie, they couldn't afford it because they had to pay a sitter. They can't travel because they don't have a car that can get them around with any kind of dependability.

And then they are tired all the time because KIDS ARE A LOT OF FUCKING WORK!

I wish I would have recorded her meltdown as it would have been a great birth control video for the health classes held right around the corner.

But let's get back to Maslow... After the basics are met, safety and security, the social aspects of this pyramid come into play. This aspect of Maslow's hierarchy involves emotionally-based relationships in general, such as:

- friendship

Jesus Has Two Daddies

- intimacy
- having a supportive and communicative family

Us homos (uh, homo-sapiens) need to feel a sense of belonging and acceptance. You remember Sally Field's Oscar speech, don't you? "You like me! You really like me!"

It's all we ever want. But for LGBT youth, this is often not an option, and it isn't until the person grows up and moves out that this part of the pyramid is met. Family and friends often reject the recently out youth, and this rocks the whole structure of the pyramid. When an African-American youth encounters racism, their family, church, and community are there to support them. When a Jewish youth encounters anti-Semitism, their family and faith community are there to support them as well. But when a young gay person is confronted with homophobia, it often comes from the groups that are there to support them. The Beatles said, *"All you need is love,"* and they were right. When this is removed, the person can be susceptible to anxiety, loneliness and depression. As demonstrated by my friends from high school. Many of them found solace in their budding sexuality, mistakenly replacing sexual fulfillment with emotional fulfillment. While they went from person to person trying to find "the one," they also managed to find HIV and AIDS and ultimately, an untimely death.

I shared this in an email to a former student, a bright, young woman who is now in California chasing her dream to be an actress. She had talked about going to see the Names Project AIDS Quilt and how it had changed her life and made her more socially aware. This is the email I sent her:

I will tell you that when I graduated from high school in 1982, the future was indeed bright for me. I had been told by some family members, community folks and the church that as a gay person, I would lead a miserable, lonely life. I rebelled against that notion, and led a life that was robust, full of friends and people who loved me. Things were going great, and then this big disease with a little name showed up. For a long time, that cast a shadow on me as well. I viewed my life as terminal (which it is, but I thought I would die early as a gay man) and held little hope for living beyond 30. When we first heard of AIDS, it seemed to be a death sentence. No one felt safe, and there was little we could do to avoid it. I was told that I would never have kids, that

15

I would never find love, and that I would die early.

So far that hasn't come true. I have a family; I have a soul mate in Tod, and I am doing well for a forty something.

While this young lady has a great deal of respect for me (and I for her), it wasn't always so. My position as a high school teacher kept me in the closet for much of my career. Oh sure, there were rumors that flew around like wild fire, but no one actually talked about it. Some students knew, especially toward the end of my tenure at the school. I led the school's diversity group. We weren't bold enough to call it a GSA (Gay-Straight Alliance), but that's what it was. We were a rag-tag group of students and staff. We were the misfits and outcasts, but we found strength and support in each other.

The Diversity Group at CCHS.

Field Observation:
From the Island of Misfit Toys (December 2010)

Ever since I can remember, I have loved the Christmas special *Rudolph the Red Nosed Reindeer*. We both premiered in 1964 and the show features two of my favorite things: burly redheads and St. Bernard dogs. The show is a classic on many levels. I have noticed that a lot of my LGBT friends love the show as well, and I think it's because of its endearing story and great characters. But there is more than that. It tells the tale of a group of outsiders, or misfits, as they are known in the show. For many of us; it paralleled our own lives as LGBT men and women. Especially our childhood. I remember hating gym in school, and the coach reindeer at the beginning of the show mirrored exactly what I endured with all my misguided gym teachers through elementary school.

Hermey, the fey and dentally fixated elf, pines for a better life as a dentist somewhere other than the North Pole while Yukon (the inspiration for our dog's name) lives as an outsider in the great, white north. And then there is the Island of Misfit Toys. So much of that concept connects with me, because when AIDS first came out in the 80s, the ultra-conservatives talked about rounding up and isolating the gays, so that the disease wouldn't spread. For a long time, as a young man, I worried that I might end up on my own little island due to who I loved and my misconceived status as a misfit because I was gay.

But, like in the show, the misfits band together and make their own family, one born out of rejection and hatred but ultimately joined in love. Our friend Michelle once sent us a Christmas card that read "friends are the family you chose."

I agree!

With all the current talk of bullying and harassment, this holiday show has a great message of acceptance and unconditional love. I may be a misfit in some people's eyes, but I am a happy misfit.

CHAPTER FIVE:
COMING OUT, AGAIN.

IT WASN'T UNTIL I began teaching at the college and officially came out that my life began to change in regards to my own personal worth and self-esteem. The next layer of Maslow's pyramid is related to these issues.

- Are you respected?
- Do you have self-respect?
- Do you respect others?

When I "graduated" from teaching high school and began working at the college, I finally came out in *all* aspects of my life. I was worried as I was on the tenure track, and I didn't want rumors or questions of my sexuality to detract from my tenure review. I had a frank and open conversation with my dean and shared with him the need for a GSA on campus. We had taken the train to Chicago for a departmental trip, and on the way home, a student came out to the entire group in the train car. The ride home was an interesting and enlightening for sure.

With the dean's approval, the student and I moved forward with the creation of the college's first ever GSA. I was having lunch with the director of Human Resources, and she was talking about my work on campus with the group. I asked if anything had been done in the past, and she shrugged her shoulders and remarked that she had been there for over 30 years, and I was the first person on faculty to be out and in the open. Certainly others came before me, but none were as out as I had become. In the past, I worked to hide my sexuality, but now, it was front page news.

Literally.

I received a phone call from the newspaper here in town, and they did a story on the student and my efforts to create the group. It ran front page on National Coming Out Day. In the past, this would have been a reason to panic, but now, I finally felt as if I was being true to myself and my identity. A high school teacher coming out is a big deal, and possibly a career killer, but a college professor, that's a different story. I was concerned more about the student, who was a little shocked at the article's placement, but to him, it was a big step toward becoming who he was as a young, gay male. The issues that plagued my high school friends didn't seem to be as big of an issue with this young man. It's amazing what a difference several decades can make. When I was in high school, the only gay characters were Billy Crystal's on *Soap* and, in a strange way, Klinger on *M*A*S*H*. Oh sure, there was Jack on *Three's Company*, but he was just playing gay.

The author as a young Thespian.
That's me, back right.

But now we have a more open society, with entire networks devoted to LGBT programming. We have the Internet, a way to connect and find out who you are in a somewhat safe environment. When I was in high school, I remember going to the card catalog in the library and looking up "homosexuality." I didn't bother writing anything down, as I didn't want to get caught checking out those books, so I memorized the general call number and headed to the stacks, turning

Jesus Has Two Daddies

a cautious eye towards the circulation desk as I came toward the dozen or so books that this particular branch had in its collection. I remember my mouth drying out as I reached for the titles—books that are now probably out of print or out of touch with modern LGBT morals and views.

If I touched them, would an alarm go off?

Would the librarian with the lunch lady arms come and beat me with the ruler sitting on her desk?

Would my parents find out?

It turned out that I didn't have to worry. I ended up working at the library and befriended one of the male librarians. He was one of the first gay men I ever met. My folks were friends with a man and I remember going to his house for parties, but that's about it for my exposure, although I do remember a lot of men in kaftans and the great bathroom he had. The tub was actually in a mini greenhouse, so you could shower or bathe in the sunshine or under the stars. Total 70s hippiedom.

The librarian became my mentor and never failed to blow my mind with the stuff he would send my way. I remember checking my mailbox one afternoon and finding a paperback book with my name clipped to the cover with this note: "See me if you have any questions." The book was Armistead Maupin's *Tales of the City,* and I could hardly wait for work to be over, so I could go home and begin poring over this new book.

As a junior in high school, there was much I didn't understand, but I took this man's advice and asked away. It was a great honor to meet Armistead many years later at a cocktail party in Ann Arbor. I brought along all of our copies of his books, and he dutifully signed each one. Our favorite inscription was "Tom and Tod wait for no man. Love, Armistead."

The librarian eventually moved out of our small branch and took residency at the main branch downtown, a treasure trove of bigger, better, and more up-to-date books about what it's like to be gay. Vito Russo's *Celluloid Closet* was one of the first books I ever checked out proudly and openly as a high school student.

I tore through Russo's book at a furious pace, mentally replaying the scenes in the many movies he discussed in the book. Mind you, this was 1981, way before the advent of video stores, Netflix, and You Tube. I had to scan my young brain for snippets of what I had seen. As elated as I may have been to find this new freedom, the words of doom that I had heard from my early critics came back to haunt me as I finished the book. It ends with a chapter outlining how all the LGBT characters die in their various films. It was a who's who of who's dead; it broke my heart when I read it.

Was this my future?

Was I to die a tragic death as well because of my sexuality as these movie characters in Russo's cinematic morgue did?

Finding self-esteem and self-respect wasn't easy back then, and for the generation before me, it was probably next to impossible. But things have changed for the better, and thankfully, the black cloud of what I had been told as a young gay man has since been lifted.

Chapter Six:
A Look Back

As a young man, I worked at a variety of jobs, including being the Social Director at a posh nursing home in Perrysburg, Ohio. It was a private pay facility, but we had a Veteran's contract, so a small percentage of our residents were veterans. During this time, I was still living with my parents and attending church with them each week. A rather loud and obnoxious member of our church (who is probably a member of the Tea Party now) would verbally harass us young adults each week, cajoling us for being in college and not "doing anything" in his stunted vision of life as an adult. Due to his family's status in the church, we usually blew him off and laughed while he called us worthless one hundred different ways each week.

Was this bullying? Probably, but we were young, and no one seemed to care that this guy could verbally abuse us every Sunday and get away with it. Everyone, including my parents, seemed to think it was okay. I think they actually sent me to ex-gay camp at his house when I was a kid to knock out some wood working projects and tinker on cars (which I hated) since I didn't embrace any of that as a kid. This guy grew up with the Toledo mentality of post high school plans, which, even in the 80s seemed rooted in a post-WWII Boomer mindset.

If you were a girl, you had these options:

1. Get a job in a factory and hope your future husband makes more money than you do.
2. Go into the military.
3. Get the Mrs. Degree (read: get married and have kids and don't do anything).
4. Go to college? Only if you were going to be a teacher.

For guys, your options were:

1. Get a job in a factory and hope your future wife didn't want to go to college or have too many kids.
2. Go in to the military.
3. Go to college if you are going to do a useful and manly job like engineering.

And that was it. So this big guy (and I do mean big… He was physically large and intimidating and wore a flag pin before you *had* to wear one post 9/11) would pony up to us youngsters in the narthex of the church and smack our shoulders and ask us what we learned in college as he wiggled his hips and made funny faces. If he didn't do that, he'd ask us what we had done for our country lately, insinuating that since none of us were in the military, and the answer would be nothing (he was a veteran, natch).

It came to me that I could finally respond to his annoying question of "What have you done for your country this week?" Suddenly my work at the nursing home provided an answer. I worked with a group of veterans each week. We'd do puzzles, smoke cigars (yes, they could smoke in the facility, and drink too), or we would watch old war videos that I rented from the library. The VA made sure that these guys had my full attention for a couple of hours each week. For those that couldn't get out of bed, or were too far gone, I'd sit with them and read them a story from a *Reader's Digest* (which seems to be the ONLY reading material you can find in nursing homes), or I would read their mail to them. For the ones that were unresponsive, I didn't know if what I was doing got through to them at all. I could have read the phone book (probably more interesting than *Reader's Digest*) to them, and they wouldn't have known or cared.

So one Sunday, I had finally had enough. When the guy came up and started talking to us, the question came up, as it had so many Sundays before: "What have you done for your country this week?" I turned to him and started listing all the things I had done with the various veterans in the facility, calling each of them by name and mentioning what I did with them and how much time I spent with them. I looked him straight in the eye and said, "How about you?" He didn't have an answer, and from that time on, the bullying subsided.

Field Observation:
An Aging Club Kid Speaks (September 2011)

No, we weren't trying to be ironic, it was the 70s

I often get laughed at by my students for my musical choices in the classroom/studio. I won't lie; it was a tough time growing up musically. I grew up at the end of Led Zeppelin and the beginning of Abba. My choices were limited for sure. But music was a huge part of my growing up. I loved Elton John and some of the musicals my parents had on vinyl. I remember coming home from camp in 6th grade, and my parents had bought *A Night at the Opera* by Queen, and it blew my little 12-year-old-head. Apparently they needed a rock and roll soundtrack for the bacchanal they had while I was away at camp.

My early years as a young gay male and the world of music that opened up to me in the clubs, bars, and discos in Toledo had a lasting effect on my musical tastes as an adult. If I wasn't sneaking in to the gay clubs and dancing to late disco or early house, I was at the straight clubs shaking it to the grinding funk and R&B that populated the playlists at such bars like Renee's, one of the true discos left standing after the 70s. They tried to update the place with new lights and décor, but it was what it was, an old disco tucked in a shopping mall. It didn't last long into the 80s. I had older gay friends who tried to turn me on to the various musical genres taking hold, an array of music that still has a place on my iPod today. Cutting-edge groups like Kraftwerk and divas such as Sylvester and Grace Jones still rock my world. But as the 80s closed up and we moved on into the 90s, club culture was still booming. Bars were a place of refuge for my friends and me, both gay and straight. They were places where we could go and get away from it all. Sure, we had the disco anthem *I am what I am* (by Gloria Gaynor if you didn't know) to help us feel good about ourselves, but it was no *Born this Way*.

Many of my current students go to the Necto in Ann Arbor, MI another grey lady from the disco era who has managed to survive into this new century. Of course, we knew it as the Nectarine Ballroom back then. It was a spacious and opulent place where the music was amazing and every night, gay or straight, was fabulous. Money was saved up each week for the nights out in Michigan. If we drove fast, we could close the Nectarine at 2:00 a.m. and drive back to Ohio to close out Buttons or Bretz and continue partying until 4 or 5 am.

I caught the documentary *Maestro* on IFC, and the film has been floating around in my head since I watched it. I have watched the opening credits many times, as the narration over the thumping house beats brought back many memories for me. As the credits roll, a voice begins to speak:

"I want to tell you about walking into an oasis."

"Feeling like I just walked into my family's living room...it was about being safe from the social restrictions of the outside."

"Everything the Moral Majority told you couldn't do, it didn't exist anymore."

"It was a family that had only one rule, to love thy brother, and that was okay."

"It was you and them against the world, and we survived together."

I get goose bumps as I read these words because that is how I felt about going out to the bars and clubs in my early 20s. It was freedom from a world of AIDS and HIV and from the crap going on in my head as a young man who knew he was gay but didn't know how he fit into the world. The last line says that we survived together, but in reality, we didn't. I lost so many friends from this time that it breaks my heart to think about them and their lives, cut down so quickly. My nights of going out and clubbing are pretty much over now. It's a totally different experience to dance with a kid in your family room to the Wii and not be in a club. The smell of pot and poppers are replaced with the smell of juice boxes and a not so fresh diaper. I can still crank out Lady Gaga with the kids and on cue they both raise their hands in the back of my car as Mother Monster commands them to "put their paws up!" And I can still put on my headphones, grab my dog, and go out for a walk in the park jamming to the tunes that made me who I am today. The strobes are gone, but the memories remain.

Chapter Seven:
Going to the Chapel

For many, weddings are an exciting time. For me, they are a reminder of my second-class status as a gay man living in the United States. Many of the dreams that are readily available to our heterosexual counterparts don't come easily for those of us who are gay.

When I first came out to my family back in the 80s (I was 16 years old), some of the first comments and criticisms from my folks were that I would never have a family, nor give my parents the coveted grandchildren they so desired. It would seem that by being gay, my life would be one big orgy of self-indulgence and debauchery. I will admit that for a young man without many role models in my life, their rather glum forecast did seem to be my destiny. I knew a few older men who were gay, many of whom became mentors and role models in my life. Some, however, never made it out of the 80s because of illness or suicide.

My parents are now both in their seventies and over the past year or so, both Tod's parents and my parents have lost friends from high school and from their professional/work life. A phone call from my folks had my dad lamenting that his friends are "dropping like flies" as he had lost several high school friends and his long time business partner within the past six months. My mom lost her best friend from church in a sudden (but not unexpected) death. I am not denying the fact that this is a hard thing as my mom's friend was a great friend of our family and a big supporter of MY family. But what makes me sad is the fact that many of my friends from high school and my early college years never made it to the 90s. AIDS took out a large part of my graduating class' sizeable lesbian and gay population. When Tod and I went to see the NAMES Project AIDS Quilt in Washington, DC, I stopped dead in my tracks when I looked down on a block of panels from the Toledo area. I recognized six out of the eight names stitched together and fell to my knees in grief.

I wish my friends from high school would have lived to see their seventies. My friend Christopher, a lovely and tortured soul, was the first of my friends to die of AIDS. Ed, a fellow musician (from my early high school marching band years) was the first person I went to see in the hospital. The regular hospitals in Toledo didn't know what to do with him, so they sent him to the Medical College of Ohio. I had to visit him in a quarantined room; it was horrifying. But there were others. Others, who in the drug and alcohol fueled frenzy of club life in the mid-80s and early 90s, never made it to the turn of the century. While we may have shaken our asses to Prince's *1999* on the dance floor, a lot of them didn't live to write that year on a check.

I miss Tam and his partner Tom, forever stitched together on the quilt. I remember gasping for air when they showed up shirtless to work on my parents' lawn. They owned a B and B in town and a landscape service as well. I busily checked my hair and made iced tea for these two hot (umm, literally and physically) guys. I knew we would be friends, and after I brought out my cool offerings, our friendship began.

I must confess that I miss my buddy Steve the most. He was my Big Bubba BFF from Texas. I loved Steve and his genteel southern drawl. When he got sick, my family helped me through it. He was one of the first people my parents knew who passed from this horrible disease. A copy of his quilt square hangs in our attic family room, a silent witness to all the craziness our family exhibits each week. I wonder if he is somehow watching and shaking his head. I get a Christmas card every year from his mom. I treasure it.

Then there are those who disappeared, for whatever reason. We didn't have a high school group (aside from Thespians) that connected us, and many of the bars that we hung out in together are history. Yes, Facebook provided me with some great reunions, including my first boyfriend. But searches for many of my friends have turned up nothing. It's saddens me that they are gone. I have some pictures, but for the most part, they are hazy memories floating in my head. So yes, I mourn with my folks and their losses, but I hold a candle that has been burning for almost 30 years in my heart for the lives that ended much too soon.

I miss you all.

Field Observation:

Notes on Marriage from a Friend (March 2008)

Our friend Virginia penned this amazing letter to the editor to our local paper. Virginia is a member of the "old guard" here in Jackson, which tends to be rather conservative. I was not, however, surprised to see this letter come from her. She is a retired teacher, social activist, and all around great woman. My grandmother passed back in 1999, and although she'll never be replaced, Virginia certainly helped fill the grandma void. She spoke to me at church one morning after her husband had passed and wanted to know about our situation. When I explained what we had to do to secure rights to each other in the time of need and to secure our adoption with Anna, she decided to write the letter. Here is the letter: Same-sex couples should be allowed to marry:

Having recently lost my husband of 66 years, I am acutely aware of the status of marriage in this country. Everyone hopes to find someone to love, and I was one of the lucky ones. I was with him at the end and was consulted on medical decisions. And as a widow, besides a lifetime of fond memories, I receive his pension, Social Security and health care. Sadly, not all couples benefit from this arrangement.

Marriage traditionally has been defined as between a man and a woman. But from an historical perspective, the sanctity of marriage has not always been recognized as it is today. Before the Civil War, slaves could marry, but they couldn't prevent their loved ones from being sold and sent away at the whim of the plantation owner.

It took another century to give full rights to certain minorities. Since then, when justice was denied, we have revisited those inequities, e.g. Brown

v. Board of Education or Title IX. After all, this country was formed with the intent that all citizens are treated equally.

It is time to address same-sex couple discrimination. Some states have rectified this by recognizing gay marriage or civil unions. Unfortunately, this is more than a question of semantics. This union must be a marriage, legally binding and recognized in all states, that extends status and benefits to one's life partner — something we in the heterosexual community take for granted.

Not only was my marriage not "threatened" by extending this right to same-sex couples, I see it as a validation of the institution of marriage, a sign of monogamy with a binding commitment between two people. It is time to recognize gay rights are human rights, and to extend to all couples this security.

•Virginia Huntoon

Jackson Citizen Patriot 2008. All rights reserved. Re-printed with permission

Author's Note: Virginia passed away in May of 2012. She left behind a legacy of acceptance and tolerance and a host of wonderful memories. We deeply miss her and hope to continue her good work in the name of social justice.

GOING TO THE CHAPEL CONTINUED

I would hear about a family member or a friend getting married, and I would flinch at the thought of sitting through yet another ceremony full of all the trappings that make the perfect day: horrible music, hot churches, bad dresses, and the receptions. Oh sure, you could score some free drinks, but the whole concept of a reception makes me dizzy with disdain. While the wedding party is off getting their pictures taken or driving around town in a limo consummating their marriage, you are hustled down to a church basement, K of C Hall, or some ballroom in a hotel off the freeway.

Yes, we love it; play more Kool and the Gang!

It's like every junior high dance ever held... those first few moments in a reception hall... no one knows what to say or what to do before the bridal party arrives to the strains of Gary Glitter's *Rock and Roll Part 2*.

"Ladies and Gentlemen, give it up for Mr. and Mrs. Joe Blow!"

Uh, we already gave it up for them by coming to the wedding and buying a gift, what more do you want from us?

Sometime between the opening strains of *Celebration* and the *Chicken Dance* a group of kids, many of whom were in the ceremony, will start running amok around the dance floor fueled by sheer boredom and free pop. Gaggles of adorable flower girls and junior attendants, along with the unruly ring-bearer and his cousins will start screaming and sliding across the wood floor, diminishing the hopes for any kind of return on their rented outfits' deposit. Tempers flare as the moms are left to corral these little miscreants while the dads suck down all the free hooch they can stomach. At some point, a great aunt or some other matriarch shepherds them to get cake or mints, adding more sugar to their ADHD frenzy.

For those of us without kids, or the ability to legally marry, these events can cause great strain and stress. The stress is caused by the desire to strangle all the kids running around and the wish to choke the DJ to death with his mic cord. Would it kill them to play some Madonna? The strain comes from clutching the chair legs every time one of the parents chirps about how cute the kids are and then tucks back into their drink or third piece of wedding cake, oblivious to the carnage those little monsters are bringing to the hall.

In 2005, our friend Michelle invited us to her nuptials east of Detroit, so Tod and I had time on the lengthy drive over to discuss a whole host of subjects. One thing I love about Tod and our relationship is that we can talk about anything for any amount of time, or we can say nothing at all and be completely comfortable with the silence.

On the drive home after the ceremony, Tod and I began a lengthy and exciting discussion about expanding our family. We were in a new house, one that called out for more than two inhabitants. We bounced questions off of each other and grew more and more excited as we headed home on the freeway.

Tod Chimes In: *Shortly after leaving the wedding Tom pointed out that the reception had lived up (or would it be down?) to his expectation of countless children hopped up on pop sliding across the dance floor in stocking feet. At this point, I played the Devil's Advocate and asked, "What if I want to have children?" This was a truly spur of the moment comment as I had not been waiting for the right moment to spring the topic on him, nor had I given this concept any thought prior to those words coming out of my mouth. From there, the conversation proceeded the way Tom described it. I truly believe that as Tom mentioned, our house told us it needed a family and not just a couple of guys living there.*

We had been told that we'd never find love, marry or start a family. However, on the ride home after the ceremony, the defining moment came when we decided that this could be a possibility for us.

Field Observation:
911 isn't a Joke (January 2011)

The first day of winter semester 2011, I got a call from Tod saying that Anna was sick, and since it was a non-teaching day, I needed to go get her at school. The school nurse said she had a fever and a headache. I quickly did what I needed to do and left the college to go and retrieve the sick one and brought her home. Her desire to play on her day off was short lived as I put a moratorium on the Wii, the computer, and any other special toy. I told her she could watch educational TV, read, or draw. That was it. I know, call Protective Services.

She wasn't happy and didn't seem sick. She was occupied reading, so I got busy making food for the week in the kitchen. At some point, Anna called 911 but didn't hang up the phone. She hid the phone in the living room. Unfortunately, this had happened before, and we had gotten a call back from the 911 dispatcher asking if there was an issue. Yes, there was an issue.

It was a naughty 5-year-old.

I apologized, and we had a talk with Anna. But since she didn't hang up this time (and had hidden the phone), the dispatcher couldn't call back to check on us. I was busy working in the kitchen when the doorbell rang. Yukon was barking his head off, and Anna came in and said "Papa, there's a policeman at our door." I went to the door to see what's up. He told me that a hang up 911 call was made from our number. Out of the corner of my eye, I noticed Anna actively looking for a place to hide. I called her name and she screamed and ran away. The policeman, who thankfully wasn't busy that afternoon, took a few minutes to give her a verbal smack down. She wouldn't look him in the eye, and as I held her for the lecture, I noticed that she wet herself. The officer did his best bad cop imitation for our impromptu "Scared Straight" lecture. As I showed him to the door, Anna cried, realizing that she majorly messed up. I sent her to her room, and she spent the rest of the afternoon in time out.

One of my former students from my high school years is a 911 dispatcher, so I talked to her later that day after I calmed down. Shannon (the dispatcher) said that it happens all the time and that her kids have done it as well. They would rather be safe than sorry, so they would rather have a child playing on the phone and not need an officer than to ignore the hang up. Shannon said that the calls aren't a big deal, and they hear some great stories when they call back and get a parent. Caution though, don't ever say that you are going to beat the kid in joking, as *you* will get a visit from an officer. She said she made the mistake of telling her teenage child that she was going to kill him for playing on the phone. She got a visit from an officer for that comment; it was deemed a domestic issue.

Apparently testing our city's response system was on Anna's junior bucket list, and she is now content. We are mentally checking off the traditional milestones that kids go through so hopefully we won't actually need to call 911 for the next one.

So kiddies, what have we learned today? Even though Flava Flav says 911 is a joke, it isn't.

Word.

Chapter Eight:
Putting it all Together

When we first began talking about starting a family, our intentions were kept under wraps for a few months. I will admit that both Tod and I are pretty focused on what we do and what we want. As teachers, we tend to overthink almost everything we do. This is not necessarily a bad thing. We decided to keep our desire for a family in the closet for a few months since we wanted to test the water and see how things would float with our immediate circle of friends. We also wanted to make sure we could actually do this and make it happen before we got everyone excited and involved. We also felt it was necessary to tell our parents together, as we didn't want either one to know before the others. You know how grandparents get. We had some cursory discussions with coworkers and friends, but most conversations were information gathering, the "what ifs" of adoption and surrogacy. Tod provided me with a printout of books on gay parenting, legal issues, surrogacy and artificial insemination that I requested from the college's inter-library loan department. I remember getting an email from our inter-library loan librarian (whose name is Marian by the way, no really) letting me know that my books had arrived. When I came to pick them up, they weren't behind the counter as they normally were, so the student worker had to call Marian to find out where they were in the library. It seems that she purposely held the books back at her desk, so she could see who the hell requested this wild assortment of books. I will admit that the collection was indeed a little bizarre and could provoke some wild speculation.

After reading and studying up on what needed to be done, we decided to tell some of our closest friends. Our best friends lived two doors down from us in our town's up and coming "Gay Ghetto," and we spent a great deal of time with them each week.

The four of us decided to go to Ann Arbor for the night along with a straight couple that we picked up on the street one night during a street festival and have been good friends with ever since. The husband's tie reminded me of Fred Flintstone's wide tie, and I jokingly mentioned it to him as we passed. A conversation started, and ten years later we're still friends. We all packed into a van for the trek east for dinner and drinks. On the way over, we decided to tell our friends our intentions. Normally, we sit and listen to music or convene idle chit chat as we travel, but this news suddenly lit up the back of the van with questions and a desire to know more. I was a little surprised, but not completely shocked that the response from our gay friends was a little underwhelming. But the straight couple burst with questions and genuine excitement. I think that the gay guys thought that this might be a phase we were going through as their buy-in to it was less than enthusiastic.

I remember meeting with them for dinner one night right before Anna was born. They came to our house to pick us up, and the stroller-car seat combo that we had purchased sat in the foyer waiting to be put together. One friend reacted as if it was a snake ready to pounce and physically recoiled at the mess of parts in front of him. The other looked at me and said, "Wow, you guys are really going to do this, aren't you?" I nodded and took them up to see our old guest room that we had started to transform into a nursery. They remained a little hesitant and didn't say much as this unfolded. But as word got out, the reception amongst our friends and coworkers was one of genuine support and glee.

So let's get back to our parents. We purposely put off telling our parents because we wanted to tell them in person, and we wanted to make sure that they found out at the same time. The logistics were a little daunting at first, but we finally found a weekend when both couples could make the trip to Jackson. We couched the weekend as a chance to relax and visit and nothing more. Tod and I hadn't discussed the actual telling; we got busy with getting them settled and getting started with dinner.

It was early spring 2005, in the middle of Lent. My folks had given up alcohol for the season and were happy chatting away and drinking water and soda as we nibbled on appetizers and snacks

Jesus Has Two Daddies

before dinner. The time came for another bottle of wine to be opened (it was a family visit after all), and as the glasses were filled and my dad proposed a toast to family, I blurted out, "And to extending ours!"

If you remember any sketch comedy from the 70s, often there would be a sound effect of a needle being pulled off of a record to simulate a break in concentration or conversation. In my mental soundtrack that night, after I said that, I heard that sound bite in my head. The room became quiet, and I glanced at Tod who stared at me with wide open eyes. As mentioned, we hadn't discussed HOW we were going to tell them, but this seemed as good of time as any.

The questions started a second later as glasses were raised to drink when the parents realized that they would not be grandparents to yet another dog or cat. This would be an actual human child! My dad mentioned that God probably wouldn't mind, so he poured out two glasses of wine, and he and my mom broke their Lenten vow to abstain. As you can imagine, thousands of questions were asked and answered, and we did our best to get them caught up on our plans. They were a little upset that we had not told them earlier but were pleased that we had provided such a family centered forum for the disclosure. We told them that once this started, we were implementing our own "Don't ask, don't tell" policy, and it served our sanity well. We told them that we would keep them posted with any news, and that we didn't want a constant stream of emails and phone calls asking how we were doing, and what we were doing to start the family. All of the advice books had told us to set boundaries with our friends and families, as the questions can get overwhelming at times, especially if there isn't any movement toward a child.

As the night unfolded, many sidebar conversations continued throughout the house. Photo albums were brought out and dusted off and memories flowed as the news of this developing chapter in our lives unfolded. We also began calling our parents Grandma and Grandpa, and they seemed pleased with that title. My mom retreated to the kitchen to do some unnecessary cleaning, but I think it was actually a chance for her to process the information and consider how she would deal with my brother and his wife who were also attempting to adopt. As I came into the kitchen to check on her, she came over with tears in her eyes and gave me a big hug, the kind of soul-grabbing hug that is given at funerals, births, or weddings. She looked up at me and told me that I would be an excellent dad and said that our yet to be born child would be damn lucky to have me as a parent. She asked me if I had told my brother. I told her that I had not, as we wanted to tell them first. She steeled her jaw and said, using her best sotto voce, "You need to tell him."

As with much of Anna's birth and adoption, we needed to deal with the good and the bad. The issue of my brother would haunt the entire process.

Field Observation:
Scissor Sister (August 2010)

With a girl in the house, we wondered if we should cut our own hair at home, worrying that Anna would see it and take tonsorial matters into her own hands. For the past few years, she's done well listening to our admonishment to only let Teresa (her stylist) cut her hair. We have grown her hair out since birth, since she has rock star curls and her hair is amazing. But in the immortal words of VH1's *Behind the Music* "that all changed" one night. As an art teacher, I have tried to instill in Anna respect for materials and media. She has had art supplies at her will since she was able and has done well. Sure, we've had a few accidental tagging of various furniture pieces, but for the most part, she's done okay with her supplies, including the scary scissors. We cringed when her well-meaning preschool teacher gave her a pair of scissors that actually cut shit up, but she (Anna) promised that she would only do good with the new tool.

Until that night.

Her first day of kindergarten went well even though the bus was late, and I ended up taking her to school on my way to work, but things seemed to be okay.

Jesus Has Two Daddies

However, that morning (day two) we woke up to a pile of hair in her bedroom and denial of any wrong-doing on her part. Apparently a "friend" came in and cut her hair for her, so she remained blameless of any wrong-doing with this event. The "friend" gave her a rather un-styled mullet, the kind you see at county fairs or in a Die Antwoord video (Google it okay? You're welcome). Thankfully, my former student Teresa is one of the owners of a great salon downtown, and we put up the signal this morning. Her amazing team went to work that afternoon and un-styled the mullet. In the timeless words of Tim Gunn, they "made it work." It's short; it's sassy; it's kind of Meg Ryan, but it looks nice. Someone asked me if we kept the hair for Locks of Love, the short answer is NO. Anna cut the hair so crazily that none of the hairs were the same length. I don't know too many punk preschoolers on chemo, so the hair went into the trash instead of a wig.

One summer, a young girl who came with her two dads to Rainbow Families Great Lakes annual Family Week (www.rfgl.org) had done a similar deed with the scissors. She ended up needing a *very* short haircut that made her look like a boy. She spent most of the week yelling "I'm a girl!" at the top of her lungs to the boys that tried to engage her in play at the various events that week. Anna still looks like a very cute girl. Tod hates it, but I think he missed out on having the giant Barbie head as a kid to style and play with and is using Anna as his own surrogate Barbie head. I am thrilled that I don't have to mess with the screaming and the yelling as I comb her hair each morning. And yes, I am the *only* one who makes her scream when I do her hair. I followed all the rules for dealing with kids' hair, but each day that I came at her with the brush, the screams started. Many times the screaming started before I touched her. So now her golden locks are gone, but she is still amazing, and even if she was bald, I'd still love her to death. And, for the record, I did *not* sneak into her room that night and cut her hair.

42

Chapter Nine:
Faith and Family

There was one more "person" to tell, and that was the church next door. I had been involved with the city's PFLAG (Parents, Friends and Families of Lesbians and Gays) group, and worked with them to identify LGBT friendly churches in the area. Each of us PFLAGers was dispatched to a church with a set of questions. Since we lived right next door to a United Methodist Church, I volunteered to go and talk with the minister. I had ulterior motives; I also wanted to see if this church might be a match for us to join as a couple. We both were brought up in homes with families that went to church. I went to a Congregational church and Tod a United Methodist. Each of us had fond memories of Sunday school and youth group and we wanted our child to have that the same experience. Some of the most profound moments of my youth were with my church's youth group. I still talk with my friends from that formative time in my life, and the memories are strong. They aren't always the best things to remember, but they made me who I am today.

The United Methodist Church's motto is "Open Doors, Open Hearts, and Open Minds," and this was one of the reasons why we were drawn to the church next door.

Oh, and it was *Right next door!*

We were the Gladys Kravitz to the church, keeping an eye on it from our windows and defending it from any trouble makers in the neighborhood. As I sat with the minister, she listened to my questions and answered them all with great candor, tossing them back to me as questions for my own reflection; a trait that I thought was reserved for us college professors. We discussed the controversy surrounding a Lesbian minister who had recently been de-frocked for a variety of violations in the church's eyes, and she assured me that even though the UMC had some provisions that were decidedly anti-LGBT, this particular church was open and accepting.

After I completed my "official" PFLAG business, I asked her more personal questions, with the focus moving toward us joining the church and starting a family. We were welcome, and our child would be as well. The question of baptism came up, and the pastor shook her head at me and said, "Who in their right mind would keep a child from knowing the Lord?" With that information, we moved to join the church, and on a humid Sunday in August, we stood before the congregation as a couple and joined the church with our sponsors behind us.

The process of adoption can be grueling, both from a financial and emotional standpoint. Many couples never make it to parenthood because they end up in divorce court before they are able to make family court to seal the adoption. We reached a point in our search where things seemed grim, but we carried on and did what we could to continue. I slipped into a funk of sorts, as I felt taken advantage of by the whole system. What leads we had turned into dead ends or scams, and the money seemed to be endlessly pouring out of our pockets.

The church had set up a prayer room in the old sanctuary at the point on our street. It was a room full of dusty artificial flowers, mismatched furniture and tacky religious artwork. It was a room set aside for private meditation and prayer. We talked to the secretary and asked if we could come in some day and use the room. She nodded and said, "Anytime, just come on in!"

So one summer afternoon, we did...

It felt odd at first, but once we entered the quiet church and headed toward the room, any strangeness disappeared. I remember the first time I prayed with Tod. It wasn't rehearsed. It happened one night before a meal because some event going on in our life was making us crazy. I thanked God for all He had given us and then asked for help. That night started us praying before meals on a regular basis. As corny as this may sound, I think that doing that simple, but yet profoundly personal act brought us closer together. I know it did that afternoon in the prayer room. We read a few prayers that I had tucked away in a book, prayers that looked beyond us a couple and asked for help on a global scale. These were prayers that took away the me-focused aspect and made it open to all possibilities. What we did that day was give up control. As mentioned, we're teachers, so we're used to and expect a certain amount of micromanaging in our lives and our work. But we knew that if we were going to survive this, we needed to let go and to let God do His work. It was both a test of faith and a test of our will to make this happen. Did we give up?

Not at all.

What we gave up was our desire to control and the frustration that it would bring, especially with a task as Baroque as adoption. As we prayed, we relinquished control and asked for divine guidance, and asked for strength and for the ability to talk and communicate as a couple. We ended sitting in the room, silently holding each other's hands, offering up our own prayers. I don't remember what I prayed for or what I even thought, but I knew that in my heart this was the right thing to do.

While this book wasn't written to be a religious testimony, this aspect of the story bears sharing, for in my opinion, it was a watershed moment in the quest for parenthood. Our faith had been tested; our hopes had been dashed, but we remained strong in both our faith and our relationship with each other. It is my hope that as the days and years go on, we'll have moments like this when we can sit down and let it all hang out spiritually with each other and our family. For several years, this church played an important part in our life, but the United Methodist Church ultimately made a decision that would have us leaving the church that helped us get this whole thing started.

That decision came in 2008. The emotional fall-out on all sides was palatable as we worked through our feelings and the ramifications of what we decided to do.

This was our initial letter sent after much discussion and many tears:

Dear Church Family,

When we moved in to the house next door, we were greeted by many of you asking us if we were looking for a church home. From the "Open Hearts, Open Minds, and Open Doors" slogan, to the

P-FLAG information in the narthex, we truly felt that we could make a home at this church. Over time we were made to feel loved and accepted, and it became our new church home. Even before we made the decision to adopt our daughter, Anna, we wanted to find a church that reminded us of the respective churches where we grew up. This church was that church home for us. As we went through the excitement and frustrations of waiting to adopt, as well as the indescribable joy of adopting Anna, we felt the love and joy of this church and its church family. From the shower that was held for Anna Laura, to the celebration of the sacrament of her baptism, we truly felt like we belonged and were accepted as members of this church. Because of this, you will always hold a very special place in our hearts.

On April 30, 2008, the General Conference of the United Methodist Church voted on an issue that had a very strong implication on our ability to serve this church, as well as truly feel accepted as a family and as active members of this denomination. Unfortunately the General Conference let us down. The "Open Doors, Open Hearts, Open Minds," motto was put to a test and hearts, minds, and doors were closed by this conference vote. The official stance that was upheld is that no one who is gay shall be appointed to serve in the church. Although we have never felt such sentiment, it makes it difficult for us to support and serve the United Methodist Church as a whole. Christ never once spoke about homosexuality or LGBT issues, but He was rather firm and vocal on His stance on divorce. It is ironic that the UMC supports and welcomes divorced members as both leaders and as clergy, but yet rejects LGBT people for service and leadership. This church has benefited from many individuals who have dealt with divorce and the tragedy that it brings as persons who have had an active role in leadership and in worship. Christ's love and grace is unconditional, open to all who seek Him. The UMC has chosen to not demonstrate the same level of compassion and acceptance to those who are LGBT.

It is with broken hearts that we will be leaving the Church and the family we have grown to love in search of a new church home that we can physically and financially support, and a denomination that preaches God's love and acceptance to all, above hurt and condemnation. We pray that in the future the United Methodist Church will stand behind its motto and welcome all of God's children to worship and serve their church.

In God's love, for all,

Tom and Tod

After we left, it came to our attention that they held a meeting to discuss our decision to leave and what the congregation could do. We did not attend the meeting, but we were pleased to hear that they were being proactive in their response. However, we could not put our faith or our church attendance on hold while they worked out how to respond. This is our letter in response to the news of the meetings and an update as to where we stood last year.

Dear Church Friends and Family,

We would like to take this opportunity to thank you for meeting to discuss our leaving the church that we called home for four years. Although the meeting wasn't specifically about us, we appreciate it for your intentions and concern. We completely understand and love the fact that you all have been such a supportive and caring place for us to worship and socialize, and we realize that this church does not share the same views of our incompatibility that the larger United Methodist Church as a whole does... but we are still compelled to leave for a church body and governing body that finds us compatible and acceptable as ministers regardless of our sexuality.

Were this three years ago, we would probably stay and put up a fight, but now we have a child, we decided to move on to more inclusive and non-judgmental grounds.We look forward to being good neighbors and good friends. Please know that our hearts will always have a special place for you all and the church. We fight for so much as a gay couple on a daily basis, so to continue that fight into a house of worship each week seems a little daunting and against the whole purpose of worship and praise to our Creator. It was mentioned that if we leave we can't fight, but we have found a church where we don't have to fight, and we like that. We will continue to pray for the church, its many missions and members, and we hope that one day the UMC will reverse this needless and discriminatory aspect of the book of discipline.

Until then, in Christ's unconditional love,

Tom and Tod

After leaving the United Methodist Church, we shopped around town for a new church. We test drove a few, kicked the pastoral tires on some others and finally ended up meeting the interim minister at a United Church of Christ /Congregational hybrid in downtown Jackson. Prior to our move, we met with the interim pastor, and she recommended that instead of leaping into a new church, we take a break and see what we wanted from a place of worship. I am beginning to think that her advice was a good idea.

We were excited by the prospect of the new church, and got busy working on committees. We officially joined the church on Easter Sunday and could now vote and have a more active and hands on role in the decision making process at this new place of worship, something that we could not do at the UMC church.

We had some amazing moments at the new church, but then some events happened that put me right back to where we were a few years ago when we left our original church. Comments by the pastor made me feel like a second class member (although he said that was not his intent), and the soul-crushing committee stuff left me feeling cold and not connected with the congregation or its mission. I bowed out of all of my committee commitments and did not go back. Call me Morales from *A Chorus Line* because these words were ringing in my ears on Easter Sunday one year after we joined:

And I said..."Nothing,
I'm feeling nothing."

A Look Back:
A Martha Stewart Christmas:

YESTERDAY WAS A PERFECT Christmas day if there is such a monster. It was as if Norman Rockwell and Martha Stewart mated in a holy union of holiday perfection over our house. Christmas Eve and Christmas Day were great here in Jackson, Michigan, and I think one of the reasons why is that we are looking at Christmas and the holidays through the eyes of a three year old. I will admit, Anna wasn't much fun her first two Christmases. Babies are boring and decidedly not festive.

Me with the Big Guy.
I got chicken pox several weeks later.

Eat, poop, sleep, and repeat.

While for some, that may make the perfect holiday, it doesn't do much for me. This year, it was magical. We had a fine meal on Christmas Eve and then headed out to the "Night Lights" at the fairgrounds. It's a drive through light show that is pretty cool. Anna was released from her car seat and got to roam around the car as we drove through the display. We headed then to our church for a candle light service where we were tapped to light the final candle on the advent wreath. It was quite an honor considering we were new at the church. Anna slept through the rest of it, even as the organist blasted a thundering *Joy to the World* from the 100-year-old pipe organ. We put her back to bed after reading *The Night before Christmas* to her, and we sat as a family in front of the fire and drank wine.

We had a few hours of sleep and then the fun started: presents, talk of Santa, and more presents, all while a gentle snow fell outside. I had to check myself a few times to make sure I wasn't dreaming. While some of you are probably rolling your eyes and throwing up, I have to say, it's about fucking time that life goes right at Christmas because many of my memories of this holiday are damn awful. Let's review…

- The first few Christmases after Grandpa Oakley died back in the 70s, Grandma Oakley didn't drive, so she ended up taking the bus up from southern Ohio, or my mom had to make the perilous journey down to get her. To me, Grandma O was Christmas, and it wasn't the same without her at our home.
- The Christmas before my Grandpa Holdgreve died. We could see that he was not long for this world, and indeed he wasn't. You could see it in our faces as well. The pictures from that year are gruesome to look at as Grandpa was as white as a snowman.
- The Christmas my Mom was sick, and we didn't know what was wrong. The word Lupus went around, as well as cancer. It ended up being rheumatoid arthritis.
- The Christmas my boyfriend Steve got sick with lymphoma

and was in Colorado visiting his family. He had found out he was HIV positive as well, so this was not good news for anyone. I felt helpless as I listened to him and his family talk on the phone trying to keep happy tones and attitudes while in a hospital's cancer ward. And then...

- The Christmas that Steve died. The phone message from his mom said that he had "made his transition and was in a better place." My first thoughts each Christmas morning are of Steve.
- The Christmas before I met Tod. My relationship with the Latino-who-shall-not-be-named was on the rocks, and it was painful to be with my family. My brother had just gotten married with much fanfare and this was their first Christmas as a married couple. It was also the first Christmas my Grandma Oakley was not at our house for the entire holiday as she was in the nursing home. I have never felt so alone in all my life.

So humor me and allow me a Hallmark Channel Christmas just this once.

Field Observation:
iCarly *Almost Killed Eli (January 2011)*

I love *iCarly* on Nickelodeon. The show is funny and has some of the most clever and well-developed characters of any adult, primetime sitcom. However, things got ugly one night as an excited and overly tired Anna almost took out Eli's eye after watching a particularly silly episode entitled "I Fix a Pop Star." To sum up: Carly and the gang are recruited to help engineer a comeback for the self-absorbed, no talent, former child star Ginger Fox. If you just heard "It's Britney, bitch" in your head after reading that description, you would be right (and gay). I don't know the actress who plays her, but she's spot on. Carly, Sam, and Freddie do their best to get her through a rehearsal, but things go horribly wrong. The song she sings starts out with the lyrics "Hello. Is everybody watching?" and slips into delightful pop drivel from there. Anna will sometimes sing that first line over and over as she dances or when she has the toy mic in her hand. The song is annoying, but it fits the show's character. At one point during the rehearsal, Ginger gets upset and whips a fork at Freddie, which ends up lodged in his shoulder.

Yes, this is a kid's show.

I laughed at the silliness of that and Anna saw my delight so she began to sing "HELLO. IS EVERYBODY WATCHING?" and flung a fork at Eli, grazing his head, nearly missing his eye. After I regained my composure, we discussed how everything she sees on TV isn't real, nor is it to be copied. A stern talking to and a timeout were in order. However, upon returning from the timeout, another fork was flung and it was off to bed. Needless to say, we will *not* be watching *iCarly* with cutlery around again in the near future.

Chapter Ten: KidQuest 2005!

One of my best friends from my college years worked in an abortion clinic in Ohio. It seemed like an odd place to work for anyone as I can't imagine the stress level that goes on each day. From counseling to testing to the actual procedure, it's a hornet's nest of raw nerve and emotion. Yet some people are drawn to that and find comfort in helping others during this difficult time. So why even bring this up in a book dedicated to adoption and starting a family? As we began letting our friends and extended family know our intention to adopt, people began sending us notes congratulating us and wishing us well on our search. I had not talked with this particular friend for a rather lengthy time, so this news reignited our friendship and a series of emails and phone calls began. Tod and I had looked at many options prior to considering adoption. We thought of being foster parents, but that would not be a good mix for Tod as some of his students are children in the foster care system.

I had been pretty up front about my desire to adopt as I thought that it might be our best option. When I taught high school, a young female student stopped me one afternoon as I walked around the classroom and asked me if I ever wanted kids of my own. At this time in my tenure at the high school, I was not out, and this young lady's father was a school board member. I played it cool with my answer, neither confirming nor denying my sexuality. I told her that due to my bad eyes, allergies, and a family history of a million different maladies, adoption would probably be best for me. She looked at me with horror and couldn't believe that I didn't want to bring one of my own into the world. I shared with her that my feelings about bringing kids into the world is similar to my views on getting a pet. Why go out and make one when there are countless ones waiting for a home of their own already in the animal shelters? Her face continued to reflect her total disbelief as I talked about how many kids actually end up growing up in foster homes or orphanages. I gave her much to think about that day and solidified my own views long before I met Tod.

One venue that we had not explored was surrogacy, and my friend who worked at the abortion clinic knew someone who was a professional surrogate. We had done the homework on at home fertilization and knew the basics. We had one component of the mix, but were lacking the egg and womb. Tod knew that I was not thrilled with creating my own progeny, so he felt that if we were going to do this, he could be the biological father.

Tod Chimes In: *Mom, please skip this paragraph, you don't want to read it. No, seriously, I'm waiting. Okay, if you insist on reading it after I asked you not to, I then ask that you at least have the decency not to ever mention it to me. Tom had already made it clear that he did not want to be a biological father, but I did. I loved the idea of continuing the family line, so while he called around to find out about adoption, I looked into what was involved in surrogacy. Surrogacy was not going to be cheap, so before pursing it too much further we both felt I should get tested to make sure I had healthy swimmers. The first step was to talk to my family doctor to ask for the sperm count and motility test, and while it would have been easy to talk to him about it, you always have to talk to the nurse first. That was the embarrassing part for me. Tom and I are both out at the medical practice, so that added to the awkwardness of asking to have my sperm checked. Once I got past that hurdle, it was off to the lab at the local hospital. I arrived and had to explain why I was there at the registration desk and then again at the lab. There had to be an easier way. It would have almost been easier if I would have walked around yelling "I'm here for the sperm test!" Once I finally had the vial in my hand, I was told I could either go home and make the deposit or go into one of their rooms. I came prepared with a book of one-handed fiction, and I usually don't have a problem rubbing one out in strange places. I said I would go into one their rooms. What they didn't bother to tell me is that the rooms didn't have locks on the doors or that the nurses would continue working and talking right* *outside the door. So, with one foot wedged against the door, smut rag in hand, and no lube (it messes up the results) I began to make a sample. I did my best to block out the woman outside my door talking to one of my former students about the blood sample she was drawing and when he would receive the results. Yes, we live in a very small town. It was certainly not the easiest sample to produce, but it happened, and a few days later, we were rewarded with the news that my healthy swimmers would be good to go if we found a surrogate.*

As my conversations with my old friend continued, it became clear that the professional surrogate might want to talk with us. Phone numbers were exchanged and Tod began the conversation while I taught class one night. I came home to a lively (at least from Tod's side) conversation and was handed the phone once I settled in. I talked with the person and got her info. It was like any of the dozen or so interviews I do each year for the various faculty positions in the department. Basic information was being tossed back and forth as well as memories of my time in Toledo and the clinic. Many years ago, the Latino-who-shall-not-be-named and I stopped by the clinic one night to join the staff for of drinks at a local downtown bar. We knocked on the front door of the clinic and waved like idiots at the security cameras. Since this wasn't a regular business hour, all of the workers were in the back of the clinic in the lounge and didn't hear our knocks or see our waves on the security monitor. We walked around to the back of the building to try and get someone's attention, and boy did we ever. It was winter, we were both dressed in black, and had hats on. As we climbed the steps up a fire escape to knock on the window, one of the workers saw us and immediately stood up, drawing a gun. It was pointed right at us. We froze in our tracks. My friend recognized us and quickly disarmed the worker and told them that we were indeed her friends, her stupid friends, but her friends nevertheless. Of course, we saw all this happening through the protective bars and reinforced glass on the windows. But it was like a scene from a movie as it seemed to happen in complete silence and slow-motion. I have only had a gun drawn on me once; I hope it never happens again.

I found it odd that an employee of a place that ended pregnancies would be in the market to create pregnancies. I began to sense a shift in the conversation as the evening wore on. The conversation went from conditional statements such as *"If I do this..."* to the future tense *"when we do this."* I halted the conversation and asked her point blank if this was a go, and she responded yes. My eyes lit up and I nodded emphatically to Tod who beamed as well. It seems that she was interviewing us as well and had decided that we were a match. We began to talk about the basics and went into practicalities. Fees were the first issue. This was not going to be a cheap endeavor. The fees were well over $30,000, and unlike adoption, the fees for surrogacy were not tax deductible.

We set up a time to meet face to face and decided on Ann Arbor. We met up at a local coffee shop and settled in for this bizarre get to know you chat. In the course of my life, I have met many people that clicked with me immediately, Tod being the perfect example of this. A connection was made almost instantly as well with this woman, and Tod and I were even more excited about the prospect of becoming parents. One task remained, and that was talking to our lawyer about the details. We set up a meeting and excitedly walked into her office full of questions and ready to get the pregnancy ball rolling. As we laid out our story, our lawyer put up her hands and stopped us. Surrogacy in Michigan is a dicey proposition for all included as Michigan law prohibits compensated surrogacy agreements. Also, the contracts surrounding surrogacy are void and unenforceable. As professionals, we could lose our credentials as teachers and our lawyer could be disbarred. The bubble of excitement was shot down that afternoon and a cloud of despair fell over the house. We went to Tod's year end party at one of his coworker's and he barely said a word to anyone. What was supposed to be our big opportunity for our child was now a felony, and neither of us wanted to deal with when starting a family.

Since it was summer, we had time to think and time to plan. We began looking at options for adoption seeing as surrogacy and foster care were now no longer options for us. We contacted an agency in

Detroit (one recommended by our lawyer), and we started the process anew. There were a million things that had to be done in order to start:

- Background checks
- Finger printings
- Mental and physical evaluations
- Financial checks

We also began working on the "Dear Birth Mom" letter and life book to share with this yet to be identified woman. We had a lot to do, and between teaching and setting up the new pottery lab at the college, those months flew by quickly. The agency suggested we attend a workshop in Indianapolis, so we booked a hotel room and made the drive down for the day. We were told upfront that we were not your typical adoptive parents. On the adoption food chain, a gay male couple was pretty close to the bottom. We braced ourselves for being the only gays in the village that weekend and were prepared for whatever came our way. When we got to the agency's office, we were greeted with a blizzard of colorful photos and scrapbook pages lining the walls. Happy couples (mostly white, all straight) were seen in their "before" kids picture and then in their "after" kids picture. The difference was usually noticeable.

Before kids: So young, so fresh, and so well rested.

The before pictures were beaming faces at a destination wedding or staged shots in front of a Christmas tree or other holiday displays. The after shots showed the same faces, still beaming but now with a kid in the picture. I looked at the faces and noticed that many of the people had aged rather quickly in the time from before to after placement. I knew parenting was rough, but damn, this scared me. We also noticed quite a few desperate pictures as well. Couples were shown hanging their stockings up on the fireplace next to a stocking with a question mark on it. Parents were shown standing next to Mickey at Disney with a shadowy space edited in for their potential child. Perky pets were dressed in costumes and held like children. We made a mental note to *not* do anything that would make us look desperate. I know that for many couples, my brother and sister-in-law included, infertility is a horrible thing to deal with. Add the stress of adoption, and it can become a frantic situation. As a gay couple, we knew we couldn't reproduce, so that mourning was not a step we had to go through. The only true mourning we had to deal with was the fact that we couldn't use a surrogate.

As the other couples gathered, it was clear that we were the only gays once again. We went in with the others and sat in an awkward circle in the conference room of the agency. There were white couples, black couples, and a few mixed couples. As we all sat pretending to read our handouts and making idle chit chat with our spouses, the presenter came in to the room followed by another male couple. The gay gods had indeed been shining down on Indy that day, for we were for once *not* the only gays in the village. The couple, a black guy and a white guy, sat across from us, and as they scanned the room, their eyes met ours, and smiles crossed their faces; little waves of greeting and excitement were exchanged across the floor.

After a brief introduction, the presenter asked us to share our story as a couple and started with the couple next to her. As the morning proceeded, we heard horrible stories of loss, stories of incredible want, stories of mourning, and stories of possible divorce. Not one heterosexual couple was there because they just wanted to

Jesus Has Two Daddies

adopt, they were all there because they could not have kids. Tales of the expensive in-vitro procedure were coupled with tales of unsuccessful pregnancies. The men were often the most shy to discuss details, but in this safe room, all cards were on the table and as the introductions went on, tears flowed and the box of tissues was passed from couple to couple.

The details of the day are now a foggy memory for me, and that's a good thing. The amount of minutia generated by adoption is truly mind-numbing. But one comment stuck out. A white couple asked the presenter what their chances were for a healthy white baby. The presenter sighed, took a deep breath, and began to lay out to us the realities of adoption. Birth moms look for a family that they think will be best for their child. They look at the life books and imagine how their child will fit in with this family. There is much speculation and acting on faith and instinct. Add to this mix the hype generated by celebrity couples adopting, and it becomes a big mess. The fact is, adoption is still a rare event in the United States, but it seems that once you "come out" as an adoptive family, suddenly everything changes, and you find out that you are not the only one. But as the discussion went on, we were reminded that we were low on the chain of desired parents. Black couples, black single women, white couples, white single women, lesbian couples, and even the mixed gay couple were ahead of us on the list. We were down so far, we wondered if anything would be left for us to start a family with. The presenter brought up the startling fact that many couples turn down children because of race, background, or special needs and that for many male couples, what was left was what they ended up adopting. We were also told that for the majority of heterosexual couples the time from approval to adoption was usually a year or less. We were told to expect to wait five to seven years. I thought that the nine months needed for a traditional pregnancy would be insane; I couldn't imagine that length of time. We briefly chatted with the other couple and left the workshop to go and tour the city. The stress started to take its toll on us as well as the heat. We stumbled upon a wine and jazz festival in a downtown park and proceeded to get completely wasted on the samples offered by the vineyards. Needless to say, that night was a blur as well, but we managed to go out for sushi and had a nice conversation that reaffirmed our desire to be parents and our commitment as a couple.

One of the more bizarre aspects of adoption is the countless questionnaires and the seemingly endless stream of papers to fill out, notarize and mail in. At one point, we had to bubble in what we would accept as a potential child and what we would not accept. This, to me, seemed cruel and more like something you would do on a dating site. Under race, we checked "any" as we knew that people would know by looking at us that we were an adoptive family. We weren't concerned that our kids wouldn't look like us because we didn't create them. We learned that many straight couples check their own race only to avoid this potentially awkward situation. Gender was not an issue either, although both of us wanted a girl. The only hesitation for us was when it came to special needs. As teachers, we both had worked with children of all ages and all abilities, but parenting was a different story. Our house was not handicapped accessible and that was a big factor for us in checking "maybe" on that part of the form. This is also reflected in how you "interview" your potential birth mom should one decide to contact you.

Our lawyer gave us a script to leave by the phone should we get a phone call from a potential parent. Here are some of the highlights from the script:

> *Thank you for calling. I imagine this must be hard for you.*
> *Would you tell me about your situation?*
> *How old are you?*
> *Do you have other children? Do they live with you?*
> *Would you tell me about the baby's father? Does he know you are pregnant?*
> *How does he feel about the idea of adoption?*
> *How do your parents or others in your family feel about the idea of adoption?*
> *What is your due date? [If you are comfortable with this, ask what race the baby will be.]*
> *How did you hear about us?*
> *What would you like to know about us, at this time?*

Jesus Has Two Daddies

Hint: Generally, we recommend that you do your best to be yourself, be honest, and be respectful of her and her privacy.
Do not tell her what you think she wants to hear, be yourself.
Do not make any specific promises about money!
Do not assume she has decided on adoption at this point. She may be researching her options. Remember– there is a birthmother out there for you–it may not be this one! She may not have too much support out there, so why not be supportive even if you are a stranger. It will be appreciated.

It was surreal. I memorized this and kept it by the phone in case I dropped the ball when the phone rang with a potential match. I didn't want to sound too rehearsed or like I was reading from a script, but there was so much information to gather, it couldn't be helped.

But this openness ultimately brought us to a young lady in Virginia who was pregnant with a boy from a Saudi father. She was white, and she knew that the baby would be visibly different, and she was pleased that we didn't check "white only" on the form that she read. She said, choking back tears that she was happy that someone out there wanted her little brown baby regardless of where the father was from. The only sticking point for a potential match was the father's faith. As a Muslim, he was not sure he wanted his kid raised by two gay men. The mom asked me questions about religion and if we would raise the child as a Christian or as a Muslim. I told her that we lived less than a mile from our city's mosque and that, when appropriate, I would introduce the child to the religion of his father. That seemed to satisfy her questioning, but in the end, the father said no to us, and with a tearful telephone call, she ended our brief relationship and one of our first bites at being parents. Strike one.

Field Observation:
Afternoons with Carter (April 2009)

All of us want what's best for our family, especially our children (whether furry or bipeds). Anna attends a weekly tumbling class for her age group called Tumble Tots. It's an action-packed class taught by a saint of a woman and her assistant. The kids basically play Simon Says for the first half and work on gross motor skills and direction following. The second half is devoted to balance beams, trampolines, and most of the kids leave each week tired and thoroughly entertained. I leave my hearing aids at home as the noise level approaches deafening at times.

Anna's BFF attends, and it's their weekly get together to play and have fun. This session, a boy with Down syndrome started coming to the class and proved to be quite a delight. He was quite bull-legged and had hard times with coordination and the finer motor skills practiced. He was also very shy, and when the teacher called his name, he would quickly cover his face with his hands and try to hide. He also had a smile that could light up a small town and was happy to be playing alongside these other kids.

The boy spoke little and used crude sign language to communicate with his dad each week during the lesson. The teacher would tell the kids what to do and then dad would get the boy's attention and sign the command to him. This dad and I were the only two men in this session's group, so we formed a quick bond and would chat while waiting for our kids to use the balance beam or hop on the trampoline. We discussed the boy's condition and what they were doing to help him get ready for school. For his age, he was pretty low-functioning and that was a concern for the family as they enrolled him in the class. They knew that he was chronologically ready, but physically and mentally he was still at about 18 months or lower. The dad remarked one day that he was happy that we had accepted his son and was grateful that we looked beyond his disability and viewed him as just another kid.

Jesus Has Two Daddies

I had to check myself, as I became a little choked up because that is what Tod and I worry about on a regular basis. How will Anna be accepted with two dads that are gay? How will she be treated by her friends and future schoolmates? Will she become the object of ridicule or mocking because of us? After I regained my composure, I realized that most of us worry about this, whether the kid has a disability or two dads. It took a young man with a killer smile and the desire to play to help me realize that fact.

64

CHAPTER ELEVEN:
PREPPING FOR THE KID

WE THOUGHT WE KNEW what we were getting into when we started the adoption process. As teachers, we had worked with our share of kids of all ages, so nothing seemed to be an issue to us. God, were we ever wrong.

We had placed ads regarding our intentions to adopt in a variety of magazines and newspapers. Our ad, in hindsight, seems a little strange:

Loving male couple seeking to adopt healthy newborn of any race. Two Dads who will love and cherish your baby—expenses paid as permitted by law. Contact toll free. And yes, we actually had a 1-800 number on our phone for this time. We had also supplied our lawyer with a box of our dear birth mom letter and our life book—the two things we created that summer to help sell us as a couple

It took us the better part of the summer to write our "Dear Birth Mom" letter. After countless edits and rewrites, this is what we settled on to represent us. What follows is an edited (for privacy) version of what our lawyer sent out to prospective birth moms.

RECIPE FOR OUR FAMILY:

START WITH 2 DADS, TOM & TOD

Our lives are so richly blessed with health and security –with a beautiful home, a big loving family and so many dear friends –it only seems natural to bring a child into our lives. When we first started telling our friends and family about our decision to adopt, we were greeted with much excitement and offers of support, quickly followed by the statement, "having a child will change your lives forever." We realize we have no idea how much having a child will change our lives but know the change will be an incredible one that will prove to be worth it more and more with every passing day. Both of us love to cook and eat, so we decided to share with you our recipe for our future family and all the ingredients that will make it work.

Add a Strong Marriage

We met in February of 1996 and have been together ever since. During the first exciting months of our relationship, we discovered how much we had in common. For two people that grew up in different states and different environments (city vs. country), it truly felt that destiny had brought us both to Jackson where we could meet. Our Commitment Ceremony in August of 2001 was an amazing day.

Fold in Extended Family

Based on our combined family histories our child will be healthy, well fed, well educated, and well loved! (Edited for privacy)

Blend with Religion

We have a strong sense of community at our church. We are blessed to have such a strong and supportive church family literally right next door. (Edited for privacy)

Mix in Work

Both of our backgrounds include working at a variety of summer camps, as counselors, managers, and health professionals. These summers provided both of us with a great deal of experience working with children and a ton of stories to share. Tod started teaching sixth grade the fall after graduating from college. He is currently starting his 16th year of teaching and can't imagine doing anything else

Stir with Volunteer Work

Summers are filled with activities and programs that keep us busy. We volunteer at the historic Michigan Theatre in downtown Jackson and are hosting a fundraiser for the women's shelter in our home. Tod and several of his co-workers became involved in the Relay for Life fundraiser for the American Cancer Society and participate each year. We believe strongly in helping to make the world a better place, especially in our town and will work to instill this value in our child.

Combine all with love

A family friend runs a licensed daycare four blocks from our home. She was one of the first people we talked to when we decided to adopt and is excited that our child would be joining the other children in her daycare. With Tom being an art teacher, we are sure that our child will have endless opportunities to find ways to express their artistic side. We both also enjoy attending concerts, plays, musicals, and museums, so our child will have a wide array of experience throughout childhood. Growing up, we both experienced not only art, but history as well. Our family trips were centered on learning more and having fun.

Sprinkle liberally with YOU!

An open adoption is important to us because we want your child to know who you are and that you chose us to raise your child out of your love and concern for your child. We want your child to know it was important to you for them to grow up well educated in a loving family, and that you trusted us to provide that for him or her. Choosing us, two Dads, as the parents is one way to know that you will be the only mother the child ever knows.

We had several nibbles with our ads, and the one family we did meet up with seemed to be genuine in their intent for us to raise their kid. The fall of 2005 brought the name Katrina to the forefront as that horrible storm devastated much of the Gulf Coast. Ironically, shortly after the hurricane, we got a call from a young woman who happened to be named Katrina. Little did we know the devastation she would bring to our lives with this one phone call. Her mom was the one who initially contacted us. She was her wingmom of sorts, checking out to make sure that we weren't some creeps with ulterior motives. After she vetted us, she passed the phone to this barely articulate 18-year-old that mumbled and grunted through our questions. We agreed to meet for dinner to discuss details and to see if this was indeed a match. They didn't know Ann Arbor very well (they were coming in from the Detroit area), so they asked if we could meet at a truck stop that they liked off of the highway. We put on khakis and a nice shirt and headed off to find this truck stop. When we got there, we realized that we didn't need to have bothered plugging in the iron, let alone taking a shower. The place was filthy, and I was a bit concerned about my health and safety as we walked in feeling like two lost missionaries. They knew what we looked like as they had seen our profile and pictures on our website, so mom immediately came up and started chatting us up and taking us over to a table. Katrina's father was there, as well as Katrina. The father of the baby was missing in action. We made introductions, and I began to look at the menu to decide what would cause the least amount of harm to my stomach. Dad was in full biker mode with jeans, a leather vest, Harley tee and a long braided ponytail. Mom was dressed in the female equivalent of business casual with a snappy suit and nice shoes. Katrina, on the other hand, wore a very large sweatshirt and baggy pants. She barely looked at us as the night dragged on and had to be poked by her mom to get answers, or comments. Mom made a huge point of talking about how fat she was getting now that she was pregnant and encouraged her to get a milkshake with dinner. "After all, you boys are picking up the tab right?"

As the night wore on, we kept focusing the questions back to Katrina's health and what kind of prenatal care she was getting, and Mom kept pushing the questions back to how much they were going to get from us and what was needed in order to make this happen. We politely referred her to our lawyer each time a question like this came up, and Mom didn't like this. She talked about how Katrina would need a place to stay and how she would need a car and how school was *really* important to her and on and on and on. We did what we could that night and left the diner somewhat convinced that we had made a match, but something wasn't quite right about the whole situation. We gave the mom our lawyer's details and encouraged her to contact her to get the ball rolling. One of the first things to be done was the pregnancy test, not one bought at the corner Rite Aid, but one done in a doctor's office. When our lawyer pushed the mom to have Katrina take the pregnancy test, she balked and told us that it was "really hard" to get that done with her schedule. Our lawyer, never one to give up, refused her questions about money and basically blocked her until the test results were in. I was home one afternoon and the phone

Jesus Has Two Daddies

rang. It was Mom, and in a quiet voice she told me that Katrina had lost the baby and that we weren't to call her or bother her ever again. I expressed our condolences and after hanging up called our lawyer. She told me that they refused to get a pregnancy test but yet were *very* interested in how to start bleeding our bank account. In other words, we were scammed. Strike two.

70

Chapter Twelve:
After the Storm.

During this time, an odd thing happened, and it was a head scratcher for us. Our life book had a random assortment of pictures representing who we were as a couple and who we were as prospective parents. Prior to taking these to press, we had our friends and family vote on the pictures they liked best and one got a consistent "YES DO IT!" from all involved. One year in Lansing, MI during the annual LGBT Pride weekend, we walked by a cab from the Who's your Daddy cab company and laughed at the large WHO'S YOUR DADDY? painted on the back of the vehicle. We stopped, struck our best poses next to the van and had a friend snap a picture. One night, an email came to us asking if we really had a van with WHO'S YOUR DADDY? painted on the outside of our vehicle.

The infamous picture.

The anonymous sender told us to answer carefully as there was a lot riding on our answer. We giggled as we wrote back to say no, we did not drive around town asking to be someone's daddy, it was just a funny picture of us that we liked. We never heard back from that person, but one night, Tod got a barrage of emails from a pregnant teenager. We answered in our typical non-committal "Please have your lawyer call our lawyer" tone and the young girl responded that our lawyers had already talked, and we were her choice to raise her child. Within moments of hearing this, we contacted our lawyer, and she apologized profusely for not getting back in touch with us sooner. It was Rosh Hashanah, and she was busy with her religious obligations. We found out that the girl's lawyer was friends with our lawyer, and after some discussion, our life book was sent to her for her consideration. We began a series of emails to her and found out that she lived in Toledo, OH, and that she had been adopted herself. She had two moms and one of them was a professor at the local university (where I went for my undergrad). She had received many life books and sorted them into three piles: lesbian couples, heterosexual couples and gay male couples. She immediately pushed the lesbian couples aside as she was interested in being part of her child's life and didn't want to be the third mom in the picture. She then selected a few mixed race couples from the heterosexual couples pile (as she is mixed race as well). She ultimately picked us because we were relatively close, and she liked our sense of humor. Plus, she would be the child's only mom. It turns out that the email we received about our alleged pimp-mobile was one of her moms making sure that we weren't creeps and driving around with that advert on our van. We would get emails at night (as she was 15 and still in high school at the time), and we would respond when we were *in* school as we were too excited to do any work. We agreed on a time and date to meet up the following Sunday. She was in the last month of the pregnancy, and the child was due soon. The fall is always the busiest time of year for us as teachers. So many things come due this time. It was crazy trying to get ready for a kid on top of that. We went to church that Sunday morning, and we let a few of our close friends, as well as the pastor know what we were up to that afternoon. As we were walking out of the church to

Jesus Has Two Daddies

head down to Ohio, our sponsor from our membership class grabbed us and took us into the minister's study, and the four of us joined hands and the minister offered up a prayer. I am not sure if there was divine intervention that day or not, but the calming effect it had on our nerves before we drove down to Toledo was truly welcomed. We chatted like nothing was going on and were actually in a good place as we pulled into the driveway, a few miles south of where I grew up right around the corner from the University of Toledo. I had driven by this street hundreds of times in my college years, but never once thought it might be the future source of my new and growing family. As we met the girl and her moms, it was like we had always known each other. The similarities between our families and what we liked, what we valued, and what we believed were amazing. Toledo has a large Middle Eastern population, (second only to Dearborn, MI), and there are many great restaurants in town offering up the cuisine from the various countries. My personal favorite is the Beirut; however, they liked the rival Lebanese restaurant in town and offered us takeout for our late lunch at their home. It was great food and brought back many memories from my time in Toledo. We had packed a few family photos for the afternoon, and when we found out the baby was a girl, we decided to talk about the names we had picked out. They all liked our choice of Anna Laura, and we continued to talk and discuss how this new child would fit into our lives. We knew that we were okay with an open adoption, and we were pretty sure they were as well. We were only 90 minutes away, and with the booming advances in social media, staying in touch wouldn't be an issue. We had been talking in adoption speak all the time since we had received the first email and were careful about how we brought up the verbalization from our daughter's birth mom that she actually wanted us to raise her child. We knew to be careful to *not* use terms like "give up" and other words that are considered negative toward the birth parent. Since we knew that the child coming was a girl, we asked if we could start calling her Anna instead of the other nebulous terms we were using. Anna's mom agreed, and I asked bluntly if we were her choice to raise her child. She paused for a moment and said, "Well, I'm the first choice, but I can't. So I pick you guys." My heart leapt, and I think I heard Tod choke up from across the room. We didn't have Anna in our arms, but she was there in the room with us, in the belly of a very pregnant and very together 15-year-old. We exchanged pleasantries and Anna's mom brought out her small pet snake. One of the first pictures I took was of her holding the snake as it twisted around her arm propped up on her large belly. I am not a big fan of snakes, but, to show my support, I touched it on its nose and moved on and tried not to scream.

Field Observation:
Mr. Hanky (December 2009)

The big question with the under seven set at Christmas time is whether or not they still believe in Santa Claus. Their belief in the Big Guy is tenuous at best as there are many forces working against their desire to believe. Children see the multiple Santas around the malls and at parties, and they begin to realize that the one doesn't look like the other. They hear things from the older kids at daycare or at school. Maybe it's sloppy hiding of presents by the parents, or a child who suddenly learns how to spell while their parents discuss P-R-E-S-E–N-T-S over dinner. Most experts agree that when the child is ready, you have a sit down and ask them what *they* believe. You neither confirm nor deny, you simply nod your head and listen.

But this particular morning presented a different problem. When do you tell your child about Mr. Hankey, the Christmas Poo? One morning, while getting ready, we let Eli play in the shower as Anna got dressed and Tod dried off. Eli likes to hang out and play in the water as it drips from the shower head. This distraction gives us time to get ourselves taken care of and to get Anna on the way to getting ready for school as well. This wintry morning, however, Eli had different plans. Instead of just playing, he used the shower as a toilet and dropped a Yule log right in the shower floor. I was still in my pajamas, so Tod was the lucky one who had to go in and clean up the lump of coal that Eli dropped while playing in the water. Since I had oral surgery several days prior, I had been on a myriad of drugs and my stomach had not been the best. I couldn't take seeing or smelling the lump of coal that he delivered to us, so I left the bathroom and began singing the "Mr. Hankey" song from South Park as I helped Anna get ready. "Papa, who is Mr. Hankey?" she asked. Her little eyes were big with wonder and excitement as she posed this eternal question to me. I had a lump as big as Eli's morning delivery in my throat as I told her that this was not the year to learn of the wonders of Mr. Hankey, and that when she was old enough, we would share in the magical story together. They grow up so fast I tell ya. It's moments like this this that make the holiday season exciting and magical. I am thankful for the story of Mr. Hankey, and I can't wait to share it with her someday in the future. Until then, the faint calling of "Heigh-di-ho" will have to wait.

Someday, my children, someday.

Chapter Thirteen:
Tentative Parents:

After meeting Anna's mom and her family, I called my parents to let them know the news. We were going to be parents.

HOMERUN!

They were guardedly happy for us, but the issue with my brother and sister-in-law weighed heavily on the situation. We had both started this quest for children at the same time, and now, since we were in the final stages, there was a great deal of resentment and anger coming from my brother and sister-in-law. Prior to this, my brother and I would talk almost daily, chatting about family events or shooting the shit. Since the process of adoption began, the calls ceased and an obvious silence hung over our family. We didn't know that this was a race, but apparently to my brother and sister-in-law it was, and in their eyes, they were losing. For many of the milestone events in Anna's first few years, they were absent, and it made for awkward questions and conversations for those that didn't know the situation. During the time after Anna's birth, we stayed with my parents, across the river from my brother and sister-in-law in Perrysburg, Ohio. I called my brother the day Anna was born and got a cold reception from him. He barely spoke, and I had to do all the talking. Sharing the birth of my child with my brother was not the happy event I had imagined. One night as we were sitting watching television at my parents' house, the phone rang, and it was my brother telling my parents that he had left a letter in their mailbox for us to read. At the urging of their priest, they sat down and put into words what they were feeling. The letter is difficult to read, even now. The pain that they felt and put into words hurt. However, I understood that they had to go through a period of mourning. I understood that they didn't have the resources that two teachers have. The comment that was the most hurtful was the one that likened Anna to a prize in a Cracker Jack box, the prize that they didn't get, and we did. She was not a prize; she was a child, and we were happy that we were picked to raise her by a thoughtful and together teenager. I resented that comment, and to this day, those words still hurt. This was not a race, and from what we were told in Indianapolis, we had already planned on being uncles before being Daddy and Papa. They mentioned in the letter their desire to be the ones to provide the first grandchild in our family, which I find odd because at their wedding, when the priest (who talked like Elmer Fudd) charged them with "freely and joyfully bringing children into the world," most of the wedding party chuckled because they were more about their pets than they were kids.

Tod and I got lucky, that's it. Eventually, they were matched with a child and spent a great deal of time with him and the birth mom, but on the night of Obama's election in 2008, while we were mourning the potential loss of our marriage with Proposition 8's passing in California, they were mourning the fact that the birth mom changed her mind and decided to raise the boy that would be their son. This set our relationship back even further and family events became more stressful. Their visits with Anna were short and sweet. Even though Tod's brother and sister-in-law were living in Europe at the time, Anna still had more time and familiarity with them than with my family. Now my brother and sister-in-law are parents to two adopted siblings. My nieces are amazing and the tattoo on my right arm is a tribute to one of their names and to one of Anna's favorite books as a toddler. Our family events are much noisier now that there are four grandchildren in the picture. The hurt and resentment has seemed to have gone away. The nice thing is that the kids never knew this all took place. To them, we're family, and that's all that matters.

Field Observation:
KISS Army (February 2010)

This past Christmas, I gave my niece a KISS t-shirt for a present, as my brother is a life-long member of the KISS Army. Hell, I would be too, if they allowed gays in the KISS Army. I mean, what's not gay about KISS?

Makeup, theatrics, THE HAIR…

In possible retribution for this gift, my parents gave Eli a Queen t-shirt (at my brother's urging perhaps?) for a recent gift giving event at our home. I love it, and I love Queen. They're like KISS but with more theatrics and less makeup. It still amazes me that people were surprised to find out that Freddie Mercury was gay.

Really?

I suppose these were the same people who were shocked to find out Rob Halford (Judas Priest), Elton John, and the guy who played Jack on *Will and Grace* were all gay as well. I remember at a very early age loving Elton John and his music, and before anyone panics, I have known I was gay since the 4th grade, well before any of this vinyl crossed my path. I came home from 6th Grade camp and my parents had bought Queen's *A Night at the Opera* and the music blew me away. I pored over the artwork of *Goodbye Yellow Brick Road* and marveled at the wonders therein. A friend at art summer school had a copy in his locker, and we would sit in the hallway at Whittier Junior High and wonder what it was all about. Music has been an important part of my life ever since I can remember, and I am working on instilling that with Anna and Eli. It doesn't matter who made the music, or what their sexuality is, what matters is that it is *good* music. So, with his held high, Eli will wear his Queen shirt, critics and homophobes be damned. The boy knows how to rock out and has been known to don a fuzzy rave hat and Anna's pink plastic Barbie shoes while raising the roof to a Romantics tune on the stereo.

My dad told me about an article in the *Toledo Free Press* newspaper and wondered if we had had any problems with Eli wearing his shirt around town. Ironically, the first day he wore it to daycare, the daycare lady's grandson (who is also Eli's bestest buddy) was wearing the exact shirt. Was I horrified? Hell yes, I pride myself on my children's diverse, eclectic, and (thanks to Tod's brother and sister-in-law in London) international wardrobe. The fact that another toddler was honing in on Eli's hipster quotient was unforgiveable.

Michael Miller, the author of an article my dad shared with me had this to say:

To this point, we have not spent any time worrying about our sons and gender roles. For starters, we are firmly in the category of those who believe orientation is decided at the DNA level; it's not a choice we are going to influence through exposing the boys to Metallica, rare steak and Robert Mitchum's "Night of the Hunter."

We have let them play and explore with death-dealing robots, super heroes, dragons, and princesses, mermaids and Julie Andrews' "Sound of Music" as they want.

There are so many child-raising factors to deal with — health, education, socialization, potty training and 1,000 other challenges — that devoting energy to being concerned about an orientation we can't control does not make any sense. I do not believe letting Evan wear a Queen T-shirt with lyrics to a song he has never even heard the complete version is going to determine the gravity of his future loafers. Frankly, it's icky to even be on that path of speculation.

I couldn't agree more and hope that more people adopt this kind of attitude toward their kids and their futures. Let the kids love what they chose to love music-wise (even if it is vomit-inducing) and let them embrace their inner Lady Gaga if they want. There are worse things they could do. And when they bring that special someone home, know that their music choices early on had *nothing* to do with it. Although, as a caveat, boys who like show tunes are usually gay.

Jesus Has Two Daddies

There are no guarantees in life, and I would hesitate to even think about demanding a perfect child. Imagine if Freddie's mom or dad had tried to change him, the world would be a less fabulous place and *Wayne's World* would suck without *Bohemian Rhapsody*.

82

Chapter Fourteen:
Prepping for the Kid Part Two

Right after we met with Anna's mom and knew we were a match, we decided to ramp up our efforts and start collecting goods for our newest family member. We heeded the adoption book's advice and kept the hoarding and nesting down to a minimum. We had felt the pain of a birth mom changing her mind several times, so we didn't want to set up shop and have to take down everything if things changed. We decided to support our local toy store, the Toy House, a place that has been in Jackson for many years. Their signature wrapping paper of multi-colored balloons has delighted generations of young Jacksonians. We knew that they had a baby department, and unlike some of the big box stores, their staff actually knows what they are doing.

So we had dinner, a few drinks to steel our nerves, and headed to the store. It was a Friday night, and we were a few weeks away from Anna's birth. The church next door had decided to have a shower for us, so they recommended that we set up a baby registry at the Toy House, so we didn't end up with 20 copies of *Goodnight Moon* or worse yet, a Raffi CD. We walked around the infant area with a glazed look on our faces, when finally an older woman came up and asked if we needed help. We told her what we were doing, and she asked us what we had at home for the baby. As mentioned, we had kept our purchases to a minimum, so we only had a few things:

- A Michigan State teddy bear (from Tod's dad)
- A collection of baby tattoos in a book, bought on the trip to Indianapolis
- A flannel shirt from Baby Gap

We shared our pathetic list with the woman, and the look on her face said, *you are so fucked*. We knew we were in trouble. She sighed and showed us how to use the bar code zapper thingy. She asked us if we had any bottles.

Nope.
Any bibs?
Nope.
Any diaper containers?
Nope.

She shook her head and started zapping things as if she were at a shooting range. We reminded her that we only had the bear, tattoos and a flannel shirt several times, and she mentally sized us up each time.

Who were these two clueless idiots?
Why were they having a kid?
Who allowed this?

She helped us get the basics, and we then moved on to the fun stuff. We both have pretty strong views on gender and gender stereotyping since we are gay, so we decided that the room would be gender-neutral regardless of the baby's gender. We had discovered a line of baby items that matched the paint/carpet in the nursery so we began zapping away at the collection of pillows, shams and blankets. Much to the dismay of our mothers, the line we picked wasn't pretty, frilly, or pink. It was a jungle theme with whimsical animals and vines.

We discovered two things when we started this process. Girls are relegated to a world of pink and pretty and boys are destined to explore, fix, rescue or kill. A walk through any store's children's area will show boys' clothing that is rugged and easy to wash and girls' clothing that requires dry cleaning and mending after each wash. Clothing that is to be worn by any child under the age of five should be machine washable with bleach (and acid) if necessary. Any gift that comes for your child with "hand wash only" or worse yet, "dry clean only" should be shoved back into the hands of the clueless gift-giver. Or better yet, let the kid wear it, take them to the ice cream parlor or park and then give it to the gifter to wash.

My coworkers at the college had a shower for us a few months after Anna was born, and as we were unwrapping the gifts, one of my coworkers kept remarking on the pink factor with all the clothing and other gifts. She knew my thoughts on all this and several months later stopped me in the hallway between classes and on a random whim said to me, "You know it's as if we want our girls to look like big, pink vaginas with all that pink and lace." Necks snapped as students walked by and overheard this conversation. I honestly didn't know what to say, but nodded my head and agreed as I walked on to my class.

It also bothered our moms that Anna didn't latch on to the myriad of dolls tossed her way those first few months after she was born. And it further pissed them off that the first thing she actually latched on to was an Ugly Doll. You can find them online and in hip gift stores, and in my opinion, they are pretty damn cool. Jeero was the first "lovey" that Anna took to, and in his tenure, he has been peed on, thrown up on, and finally left for dead in the bottom of her toy bin.

Field Observation:
Big Kid (May 2010)

We run into one of my former students and her two children at a local park on a fairly regular basis. Her boy is 3 and is very verbal compared to our Eli who is the same age and is still in the grunt and point stage. One afternoon Eli, Anna and I were climbing all over one of the play structures, and Gabriel, the son of my student, walked by, waved, and said, "Hi little girl! Hi little kid! Hi big kid!" He offered these greetings as he passed us on his way down the play structure.

It cracked me up that this boy would consider me a kid and not a parent since I was up playing with my kids and not sitting on the bench passively watching and checking messages on my phone (like Tod does). I shared this with the class that this student is in the next day and told her that her 4.0 was in the bag. Yes, I am a big kid. I admit it. I love cartoons, I love to go and explore and play, and up until a family wedding a few years back, I didn't own a suit.

'Noopy and me at the Point.

My ultimate play area is Cedar Point in Sandusky, Ohio. It is truly an amazing place with something for everyone. A lot of amusement parks are for the coaster or thrill junkies and leave the kids and wusses out in the cold but not Cedar Point. It rocks, and my inner kid comes out every time I catch a glimpse of the coasters on the horizon as we head over the causeway into the park. A group of us tagged along with a school field trip to the park the other day and had a blast. There's nothing like riding in a comfy air-conditioned coach there and back. It's heaven. I remember bleary-eyed, caffeine fueled drives there and back in my car when I lived in Toledo when I was much younger. It's nice not to have to do that.

Jesus Has Two Daddies

So we packed up Anna and some of her peeps and had a blast. Anna is a few inches short of being tall enough for the big rides, but there is plenty to keep a junior coaster junkie happy. Taking a grandparent along is a *great* idea, as two of us who were big enough to ride the big rides ditched the kids with the grandparent and made tracks for the coasters. The Camp Snoopy area is wonderfully themed, and if the kid is big enough, he or she can run from ride to ride and not have to have a parent with them. Since there are rides like the Tilt-a-Whirl and other twirl and puke rides, the kids can scramble their brains, and I don't have to risk public humiliation by tossing my lunch after the fifth ride.

So yes, I am a big kid, but the reality of the trip to the park took its toll on my body. I will do my best to retain this Peter Pan mentality as my kids grow as I truly believe that it's what keeps me young. But right now, Peter Pan is glad Tinkerbell is at daycare because he needs a nap.

Chapter Fifteen:
Anna Makes Her Entrance

As I write this, Anna's mom is packing up her house in Toledo in preparation for her move east to start grad school. Little did we know that when we adopted Anna, we'd also be adopting a teenager. This young woman and her family have become an important part of our family and how we define ourselves as an adoptive family to this day. For many of our friends, the birth parents are unknown or are not allowed to visit their children. We have an open adoption, and that is fine with us.

The two weeks leading up to Anna's birth are a vague memory. I had been named Michigan's Higher Education Art Teacher of the Year (2005), and we were off to Frankenmuth, MI for a weekend of dinners and ceremonies related to that award. It was quite an honor to receive this award, but as the presenter read off my accomplishments at the college, all I could think of was the fact that any day now, I would be a parent. I jokingly told Anna's mom in an email that I was going to wear my award around my neck on a chain like Flava Flav wears his clock. She lol'd and shared with her moms, who apparently didn't know who Flava was. These initial moments and communications via email set up our relationship with Anna's mom and define how we interact with her today. We got periodic emails talking about how Anna reacted to Taco Bell food and how she kicked and bucked in her belly after a late night splurge at the drive thru. It was late autumn, so leaves were falling, and everyone was out raking that sunny and unseasonably warm weekend. We got an email from Anna's mom while we were down the street at our friends' having dinner, but since we were out, we didn't see it. She complained that her belly hurt after raking so much and falling out of the back of a pickup truck used to remove the leaves. She signed off by saying that she would be calling her doctor, and she'd keep us posted. While we were relaxing in front of the fire after dinner at our friends' house, Tod's phone rang. It was late, very late, and much beer, wine, and port had been consumed during the course of our visit. As Tod reached for his phone, we jokingly said that if it was Anna's mom, we would need to sober up pronto so we could get our asses down to Toledo. It was Anna's mom.

She was in the hospital and was having regular contractions. There was no hurry, but since this was her first child, there was no indication of how the labor would go. Suddenly, everything was on fast-forward, and we were throwing on our coats and excitedly heading down to our house.

We had packed our suitcase for the trip to Ohio for the birth, and it sat waiting for us in anticipation of this moment. Our friend Bryan came down to the house with us to help us pack and to say goodbye. As we ran around gathering our toiletries, saying goodbye to the pets, and splashing water on our faces to sober up, Bryan packed all the things we thought we would need into the back of my PT Cruiser. It wasn't until we started unpacking the car the next day that we realized Bryan had packed several boxes of our recycling as well as the needed new baby supplies. With a Diet Coke in hand for each of us, we left under the cover of darkness to meet up with Anna's mom and her family. We each called our parents and gave them a heads up. Both were in bed and groggily wished us well as we headed south. We arrived at the hospital several hours later and made our way up to the birthing suite with a small bag of goodies for Anna's mom. We didn't know what to get, so we bought her a CD and some other knick knacks that a fifteen-year-old might like.

As it turns out, we probably could have waited until morning to leave, as the contractions that had brought her to the hospital were suddenly absent. It was early morning at this time, and Anna's grandmothers camped out on the recliner and sofa in the room. We were relegated to the waiting room and did our best to sleep in this strange, new place. There was only one other person in the unit, and as we walked by all the empty rooms with big comfy beds, we were tempted to sneak in and sleep. Instead we each took a loveseat and tucked in for a fitful night's sleep in the lounge.

Jesus Has Two Daddies

We realized it was a good call to come down even if the contractions had stopped. We knew that with the news that Anna's mom was in the hospital, neither one of us would have slept even if it was in our own bed. Earlier that afternoon, while we were busy doing nesting things, I suggested to Tod that we should probably go and take a nap, as this was possibly our last weekend to take a nice leisurely nap. He resisted, and we ended up working throughout the afternoon. I am still waiting for that nap, dammit.

We were warned by many, including our lawyer, that the Lifetime channel was strictly forbidden while we were in the process of adopting. The network's many shows on babies, adoptions, pregnancies, were great fodder for igniting fears, causing stress, and generally making waiting parents cry at the drop of a hat. Even without watching these hour long docu-dramas, we knew that our kid would not magically show up after 59 minutes to tears and hugs. As the morning wore on, we played games, talked, and got to know each other better. Random nurses came in regularly to monitor Anna's mom and check for contractions. Remember, it was only three weeks or so after that initial connection, so we were still trying to discover more about our new family. Anna's mom's boyfriend was there and stood silently in the corner for most of the goings on. He was shy and talked only when addressed by someone in the room. I should make mention here that we are not sure who is Anna's biological father. Anna's mom told us that she was sexually attacked by an unknown, white male. She hid the pregnancy until the seventh month, so the timeframe for any forensic measures after the attack had long since passed. This is an awkward situation to talk about as I am suspicious of her story. However, I respect her and will respect her decision to keep the identity of the father a mystery. At some point we may know, but at this time, we'll leave it up to her mom to disclose the information.

Anna's mom has two godmothers, friends of her moms' who had been with her since her adoption 14 years earlier. They came in to visit that morning, and as we got to know these lovely ladies, we began talking about who should be Anna's godparents. The obvious choices were our siblings, but with Tod's brother and wife living out of the country, they were knocked off the list. With my brother and sister in law's recent shenanigans, they didn't even make the list. We also wanted to mirror what Anna's mom has, godparents that were like her parents, a same-sex couple. We then thought of our friends Brian and Alan. They had been together for as long as we had and in our minds, were the closest to what we had in a relationship of all our friends. They had their wedding on September 15th, 2001, four days after the horrific attacks on our nation. The weekend before, at their bachelor party, we breezed through customs to go to Canada for a night of debauchery and strippers. A few days later, they were waiting on friends to come into the U.S. for their ceremony, stuck in the long lines of stranded internationals at our nation's borders. Their event was one of hope and of sadness as we all bowed our heads for a moment of silent remembrance during their ceremony. For most brides, their wedding ceremony is all about them. For those two, it was all about us, the collective mourning of a stunned and saddened nation. I will never forget that moment in their special wedding ceremony. After some quick discussion, they went to the top of our list. We didn't rush off and ask them that morning the time for that came several weeks later.

Both of our parents showed up that morning as well. Mine had gone to church and came to the hospital right after. Tod's had gotten up and driven in from the west side of Michigan. They had seen pictures of Anna's mom, but this was the first time they were to meet the young woman who would give them their new granddaughter. It turns out they bonded quickly with Anna's mom's mothers and settled into talk of being grandparents sometime soon. My dad has a knack for digging into people's pasts and finding out what friends they may have in common. As he talked with Anna's mom (the professor), names were batted around, and it turns out that she knew the deceased husband of one of my mom's good friends from church. We ordered lunch and retreated with our parents to the large waiting room for a meal of lukewarm takeout. It was infinitely better than the alleged food the hospital served for breakfast that morning. Being exhausted and slightly hung over, we just wanted good food. Instead we got reconstituted yellow Styrofoam and mystery meat. Both families needed this break, as the pleasantries were wearing thin

Jesus Has Two Daddies

in the birthing suite. We talked about what would take place after the birth and set the grandmothers up with the task of outfitting the new temporary nursery at my parents' house. Many of our friends have gone away too far off countries to adopt their child, many times with less than comfortable settings and no Wi-Fi. While they languished in Wherethefukistan, we set up shop in my parents' house with the help of two doting grandmothers. While they tried new and exciting cuisines, the only thing tried on our end was our patience.

A belt was secured around Anna's mom's waist and hooked up to a monitor. From this monitor came the fast and steady heartbeat of our daughter, enjoying her last moments in her mom's belly. The contractions were coming closer and closer, and Anna's mom was moved to the delivery bed. My mom worked at Toledo Hospital for much of my childhood. My dad, brother, and I would meet up with her on the weekends and enjoy lunch together. We'd wait for her in the nursery area, looking into the clinical and scary and decidedly off-limits delivery area. This was like being in a hotel room, right down to the hot tub in the corner of the suite. While Anna's mom loves all things aquatic, she thankfully opted for a non-aquatic delivery. The two midwives assured us that she was in good hands and that although the birthing wing of the hospital was pretty much deserted, there was a physician on hand should something go wrong. Everyone decided it would be best if we all got out of the room and gave them their space. Tod and I decided to go for a walk and check out the artwork in this rather new hospital. I grew up about a mile north of the hospital, and had driven by the space where it sits countless times in my youth. But this afternoon I felt like a stranger in a strange land. Rather than being a cigarette smoking art student, I was an expectant dad shopping for bubblegum cigars to pass out after my daughter was born in the hospital's gift shop. My mom called when it was show time.

We gently knocked and poked our heads in to see what was going on. Anna's mom had her feet up in stirrups, and it sounded like the ocean was right outside the window. She was in full labor and the sloshing noises coming from the monitor were Anna trying to find her way out. We demurely stepped behind the bed as her mom was spread out for the world to see with her legs up on the stirrups. "Oh no you don't!" cried one of the midwives. "This is your kid, get down here; you'll never see this again."

Two men who had not spent any time around a naked female were suddenly front row center to the show of a lifetime. Anna's head was coming out and the midwife remarked how dark and curly her hair was. "I want to see!" yelled Anna's mom, and the midwife held up a mirror for her to look into. Due to her size and the size of her belly, she couldn't see so she demanded that I take a picture. I am never without my camera, and this time was no exception. I looked at the midwives and asked if I could take a picture and the one remarked that she was surprised I hadn't already. Many new dads will show up with enough camera equipment to film a movie, recording every detail of the birth in HD. I will admit that I was a bit hesitant taking a picture of a fifteen-year-old girl's vagina, but with her permission, I snapped a picture and held it up for her to look at. I noticed a large sling set up under Anna's mom's legs and jokingly asked the midwives if that was the backup should one of them drop Anna during the delivery. "No," replied one, rolling her eyes, "it's for the amniotic fluid and afterbirth." Yes, there was blood, and yes, it was crazy nasty. Even though I am a fan of horror movies, I was grossed out by the thought of this plastic sling filled with fluid of all sorts. The even grosser part is that these are reused after being cleaned and sterilized.

Shudder.

Tod and I were never part of the Lamaze classes Anna's mom attended, but we suddenly moved in to the role of coaches as we cheered on her mom to push, breathe, push, breathe, and repeat x 1,000. The room felt electrified as our daughter slowly made her way out in to the world, covered in what appeared to be ricotta cheese. The monitor was still on 11, broadcasting a whole host of new sounds into the room. It was a circus of noises, most of which the midwife told me to ignore.

Was her heart beating too fast?

Was it beating too slowly?

Why did it just stop beating?!

We had briefly listened to the *Sounds of the Womb*, a 60 minute CD of womb-like noises designed to help your baby fall asleep faster after they are born. I began to wonder how quiet and relaxing it is in there with all the noise going on around me in the birthing suite and decided that we were better off not buying it. After much pushing, breathing, and screaming, Anna was born. At 3:35 pm on November 13, 2005. I was now a dad.

*If it wasn't for this picture, I wouldn't have
remembered any of the important times.*

A healthy baby girl was hoisted in to her mom's arms and two clamps were attached to her umbilical cord. One of the midwives had a pair of scissors and was snapping them open and shut asking us who wanted to do the honors.

SHIT!

No one told us about this decision in all of our prep work. I looked at Tod and his eyes were the size of saucers. "Not me!" he yelled and the nurse said "Get up here Papa and cut the cord!" I think she purposely allowed a little fluid to gather between the two clamps before she sealed it off, because as I cut it, blood sprayed everywhere. All my years of watching and regaling in splatter horror films didn't prepare me for this. It went *everywhere*, including my shirt, the shirt that I had now been in for almost 24 hours. Suddenly, I was Shaun, in *Shaun of the Dead* as I had a bit of red on me, a lasting reminder of that very special day.

96

Chapter Sixteen:
Afterbirth/Aftermath:

ONCE ANNA WAS SECURED and sent off for a quick rinse and fluff for the upcoming grandparent presentation, the midwives began working on her mom. She was having a difficult time with the afterbirth and the situation was not good. We were asked to leave the room, and we went out into the hallway and began chatting up the matronly nurse working behind the desk. She was crocheting a bonnet for Anna as she did for every child that came through the hospital, and she asked us if we had a problem with her putting a pink ribbon on it for a strap. We chuckled and said no, that would be fine with us. I think she thought that since we were two dads, we couldn't be bothered with all this frilly girly girl nonsense. We were touched by her kindness and her acknowledgement of our new status of parents. Everyone in the ward seemed to know our story, and it was never an issue for us to come in or visit. The morning was a blur, and at this point, I was ready to drop from exhaustion, but as we were chatting with this lady, I noticed a swaddled baby behind her in a bassinette. It slept quietly and made those funny baby-sleeping faces babies make. I hadn't noticed it before and asked what was up with it being out behind the desk. The nurse remarked that some moms want their kid with them 24/7 after delivery, but some just want to get a good night's sleep. This was the case with this little one's mom. She had gone through a pretty rough labor and was not physically ready to deal with a newborn. But on our side, once Anna's mom's health issues were addressed, Anna went right back in and never left the room. She knew that she had a limited time with her, for as soon as she was discharged, we would take custody of Anna.

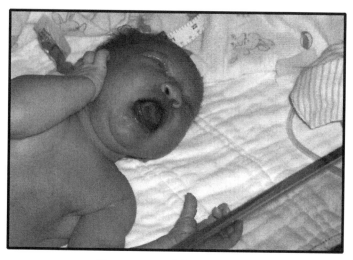

Yup, not much has changed.

After a bit, Anna was returned to us in the birthing room, and we were able to bring her out to meet her other four grandparents. Smiles and tears were on everyone's face as this bundle of baby was passed from person to person. Phone calls were made, pictures were snapped and then the grandparents left to go and ready the house for our return and for their new granddaughter. Tod and I hung out for a bit and then decided we could do no more and said good night to our daughter for the first time. We drove to Perrysburg, and we moved our stuff into the modest ranch home my parents own in this sleepy historical town on the Maumee River.

While sleeping in a yurt in Wherethefukistan would have made for a far more adventurous start, I was happy for clean sheets, hot water, and four eager grandparents willing to help us make this difficult but exciting transition into parenthood. As we ate pizza and nibbled on chips, it was all I could do to keep my eyes open. We went to bed and I remember sleeping like the dead. I don't even remember kissing Tod goodnight that evening; I remember being the happiest I had been in a long time.

CHAPTER SEVENTEEN:
HONORABLE DISCHARGE

THE NEXT MORNING, WE got up, had breakfast, and headed in to see our kid. We stopped by a store and bought a gigantic "It's a girl!" balloon and a box of chocolates for Anna's mom. We also bought a bottle of wine for her moms in celebration of their new granddaughter. We stayed in the room, holding Anna when we could, as there was a steady stream of visitors from the moment we stepped in. Anna's mom dutifully introduced us to all her friends and extended family and called us both Tod and Tom and Anna's dads. There wasn't too much for us to do, so we bowed out and left to go and eat. We were summoned back to the hospital that afternoon to talk with Anna's mom's lawyer. Our lawyer was by no means cheap, but hers was charging almost $500 per hour. She needed to meet with Anna's mom and go over some final details before Anna was discharged to us the next day. The guests were ushered out of the room and the lawyer went in to talk with Anna's mom alone. This was done to make sure that the child was not being put up for adoption against her will or that she was not under any kind of duress or threat to give the child up for adoption. Initially, Anna's mom had wanted to raise her, but due to her moms' age and the fact that she was still in high school, this was not a possibility. She had gone to counseling, at the urging of her parents and the lawyer, to help her sort out her feelings and to help her cope with the separation coming the next day. We were called in, and we grimly sat around listening to this woman talk (at $8.00 a minute, mind you) about what came next. Now that Anna was here, ads were placed in newspapers all around the area alerting the possible father that the child was being placed for adoption. This seemed like an odd thing to do, but a necessary step to terminate parental rights. Since Tod had the better insurance, he was adopting Anna first so much of the paperwork and legal stuff fell into his lap that weekend. Forms were signed, and we were ready for the discharge tomorrow. We kissed our kid goodnight and headed back to my parents' house.

This is an embarrassing side note, but one that needs to be shared. I am a huge Madonna fan and love everything she has ever done. *Confessions on a Dance Floor* was released the day we were to get Anna. As we headed into town to bring our daughter home, I made Tod stop by Target so I could pick up the CD. The 20 minute drive into Toledo was filled with the thumping retro-disco sounds of album. I figured I needed to get this listening in now as my future had Raffi and the Wiggles penciled in for listening material. The CD case is still in the pocket of my door, a reminder of just how gay I am.

In case you still aren't convinced, I dug up this old Live Journal entry to help convince you otherwise:

*Today truly is a national **holiday.** It always is when a new Madonna CD comes out. So, a few of my students were running to Michael's to pick up some art stuff, and since I am stuck here until 9 tonight, I tossed one of them a $20 and asked them to pick up **Hard Candy** for me. Yeah, I am the gay for doing that, but hey, what's a **true blue** fan to do if he has to work all day when her CD comes out? So far, I like it a lot. It's not her typical stuff, but it had us bobbing and dancing in the studio as we previewed it. We were all pretty much **into the groove.***

*The remixes will probably be killer, can't wait to hear all of them. Not sure what D.J.s are in **vogue** right now, but they certainly have a lot to **express themselves** with then they hear this. I hate to **rain** on anyone's parade, but this truly a great work of art. Certainly not **bedtime story** material, as you'll want to go and dance, but it isn't **frozen** in the 70s like the last CD. I could go **deeper and deeper** into my analysis, but I won't.*

*The day that **Confessions on a Dance Floor** dropped was the day that Anna dropped into our lives. Since we couldn't get into the hospital until 9, we dropped by a Target and picked it up on the way to take her home from the hospital. Years from now, when she reads this, she'll probably end up in therapy for that... but hey, she'll **live to tell**. I doubt she'll be too **hung up** on the fact that I put getting Madonna over rushing to get her from the hospital. We'll talk, but she'll probably just say... **Papa don't preach**.*

Yup, that gay.

Since Anna was coming home with us, the car was set up for her

Jesus Has Two Daddies

and had the base of the car seat installed in the backseat. We grabbed the car seat itself and headed up for our last visit in the hospital. Anna's grandmother (the professor) met us as we got off the elevator and said it would be better if we weren't in the room at this time. So we spun around and returned to the car and headed to a local bagel shop to eat an early lunch. Anna's mom was having a rough time with the thought of Anna leaving her today and was emotional. My stomach dropped as I had visions of us returning to Michigan without a child. I hesitantly asked if everything was okay (translation: is the adoption still on?), and the mom reassured us that it was indeed still going to happen. We got into the car and headed out for our lunch. As we entered the restaurant, I was flooded with many memories from my college years. I had eaten at this particular bagel shop many times in my years in Toledo, and the shabby retro-hippie vibe was still there. In my youth, I could never afford the fancier offerings due to my student budget limitations. Now, I could afford the fancier stuff, but my stomach was saying "NO!" as I looked at and considered what was once unaffordable on their menu.

I think this meal was a chance for the mom (now grandmother) to reassure herself that we were indeed the real deal and that we would live up to our promises regarding an open adoption several weeks earlier. We did our best to present what we thought she wanted to hear, and it seemed to be okay. We joked that had I stayed in Toledo after college, we may have actually been friends before this. I remarked that we were not only friends, now we were family as well.

We returned to the hospital, and on cue, Mother Nature decided to be a drama queen and turned the skies grey and nasty for added effect. We grabbed the car seat again and it dawned on both of us that we had never read, let alone practiced, strapping an infant into the chair. We placed the car seat on the desk and the matronly nurse from the day prior presented us with the finished bonnet and then began showing us what to do. A lot of drama came from the room as Anna was removed for a final check of stats and vitals. Tod met with the social worker, and the papers were signed, and Anna was ready to go with us. The emotion coming from the room took its toll on us all. I had a rather grim face as I watched Anna's mom cry and hug one of her moms who was also in tears. The nurse pulled us aside and said, "Hey, you guys are the good guys here, you're wearing the white hats today!" I couldn't help but feel like a villain, robbing this poor young woman of her child. But the nurse was right; this was the right thing to do. It wasn't the easiest thing to do, but it had to be done. Anna rode to our car in her mom's lap. Her mom was in the obligatory hospital wheel chair, and her mom was doing the best to balance the car seat as she was pushed down the hall. Hugs and tears were once again flowing freely as we secured Anna in the backseat of my car. I climbed in next to her and allowed her tiny had to grasp my finger as we drove off. The threatening skies turned into a full-fledged storm, and as it poured down rain and thundered, we drove off to Perrysburg for Anna's first night out of the hospital.

Anna's grand entrance in my parents' garage.

Chapter Eighteen:
And Then What Happened?

Our time in Perrysburg was rather unremarkable, I won't lie. There were some moments that were head-scratchers and caused much "Why are we doing this again?" discussion between Tod and me. One of the problems was the fact that Anna was lactose intolerant. I knew about the first few weeks of diapers and how nasty it could be, but this bordered on ridiculous. We would feed and change her and then the explosions and screaming started. My mom called a pediatrician friend and they suggested that we switch to soy formula. We did, and the change was amazing and quick.

Anna was calm, cheerful, and not a 24/7 poop machine. We were able to have conversations again and began to have not such stressful interactions with our new baby girl.

Suddenly, it all seemed normal.

We did a few day trips around the area to test-drive our new stroller and one of our stops was the Toledo Museum of Art. To define the moment that I entered the museum for the first time with my kid as surreal is an understatement. It was like a Dali/Ernst sandwich served with a side of Björk. Many times as a student, I struggled to get in through the museum's heavy doors with my bulky portfolio and art supplies now I struggled to get in with a stroller and a diaper bag. We wandered the galleries and Anna cooed and chirped as we passed the many masterpieces on display. The frantic pace that I normally set when I am in a museum (get in, see the big stuff and leave time for the gift shop) was thrown out the window as we slowed down and enjoyed our time there with Anna. I snapped a picture of her in front of my favorite Matisse, and my flash accidently went off. I was horrified as the guard came up behind me and tsk-tsk'd in my ear. I blushed in embarrassment as I reassured him that it would not happen again. As I disabled the flash, I noticed the picture that I had snapped on the monitor. Anna was facing the painting, and her mitten covered hand was pointing toward the painting in front of her. The Fauvists are a little heady for most, but apparently my week-old daughter already had exquisite taste in art.

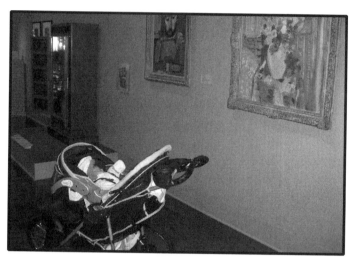

I am now on the watch list at the museum thanks to this picture.

The other problem we encountered was our moms. As teachers, we are well aware that if you do the work for your students, they will never learn. However, our moms didn't get that message, and from day one, we were chided for how we held Anna, how we fed her, how we did just about anything. Grandma does know best, but this reached the point of annoying. It was rough that first week with both of our moms there, but we were happy to have the help. The never-ending scrutiny killed us. Yes, infants are delicate creatures, but we never once put Anna in danger or physically harmed her. We had to remind our moms about this several times, and we did so with our teeth clenched, voices steadied, and our desire to strangle them in check. Tod snapped first, and it was with my mom when I was back in Jackson for work. The details are sketchy, but with our lack of sleep and new role as parents, it was undoubtedly something small blown up to something big. But after these few rough bouts, it was pretty mellow. I should

Jesus Has Two Daddies

clarify, as mellow as it gets with a newborn in your life.

Our close circle of friends from Jackson asked if they could come down for a visit. We were more than thrilled to have the company and to have some faces from our life back in our hometown. We agreed that they would come down after work and stop by our favorite Lebanese restaurant to get takeout for our dinner. When the van pulled in to the driveway, I was almost in tears (yes, we cried a lot during this time).

This was **our** support system, and they had kibbeh.

Hugs and words of congratulation were shared as Anna was once again passed around from arm to arm. Our best friends from down the street were still a little gun shy with this new addition to our family, but as the evening wore on, Anna stole each and every heart in the room, and they warmed up to her. As they put their coats on to leave, the question of when we would return came up. We were still in a holding pattern with our lawyer and the mountain of paperwork needed to make this interstate adoption happen. Since it was close to Thanksgiving, people were out of the office or were not doing what they should have been doing, so we shrugged our shoulders and said it was anyone's guess. It was late as they pulled out of the driveway, and we knew it would be even later when they returned home on this work night, but we were thankful that they made the trip and brought a bit of our life in Michigan down to Ohio.

Anna's mom had asked us to have a small blessing ceremony before we left for Michigan once the paperwork cleared. She and her minister had worked out a small service of blessing and transition to help with the change in all of our lives. Since we were ground-zero for all things baby, we asked my parents if we could do the ceremony at their home. They thought it was a great idea, and we set the date and sent out invites to a small group of family and friends. Tod and I had discussed who would be Anna's godparents, but we had yet to actually ask anyone. Our parents had their own idea of who should have the role, but we had decided on Brian and Alan. We asked them to join us for the blessing ceremony, but left our intention out of the invitation. When they arrived, I whisked them into our empty bedroom to pop the question. I was in tears, partly because I was exhausted and partly because it was a pretty big thing. Without hesitation, they said yes. The assembled crowd was raucous and noisy as the Ohio State Buckeyes had just won the football game against their arch rivals the University of Michigan Wolverines. Since this was Buckeye country, Tod, a U of M grad, was taking a lot of heat and ribbing. I pulled Tod aside with the newly christened godfathers and shared the news. That afternoon, a new branch of our family took form. I was saddened by the fact that my brother and sister-in-law chose to stay away from this important event, but as the year wore on, their absence became the norm. While Tod's brothers' family had the excuse of distance my brother had no excuse but his own hurt feelings. As I celebrated the birth of my daughter, I mourned the passing of a deep and abiding friendship with my brother.

The service took place in my parents' living room. Thankfully the game was over, so the television was turned off, and the minister assembled the key players in front of the fireplace. Scripture was read, and the word of God, spoken to the prophet Jeremiah, set the tone for the blessing:

> *Before I shaped you in the womb,*
> *I knew all about you.*
> *Before you saw the light of day,*
> *I had holy plans for you. (Jeremiah 1:5)*

What was God thinking by placing Anna with us?
Was this the right thing to do?
Were we the best choice for this situation?

My role as the resident Doubting Thomas and the doubts about our fitness as parents bothered only me that day, as everyone else nodded in agreement as the minister blessed and praised this adoption throughout the service. A prayer was offered up for Anna's biological father, and the minister asked that he be comforted in the fact that he will never know this wonderful blessing of a child. I steadied my eyes on the minister and did my best to not look at Anna's mom's boyfriend standing in the back of the room.

It seems that United Methodists are creatures of ritual and recitation, so this ceremony had moments of that in its design. The most profound for me were the charges set forth to Anna's mom in her discharge to us as the parents of Anna. While this wasn't an official baptism (that would come later), the minister made sure that we were ready for the duties of parenting and ready to make sure that we would keep Anna's birth family in her life. I felt like we were six and asking for a puppy:

"Will you take care of it?"

"Will you feed it and clean up after it?"

"Puppies are a lot of work you know!"

Yes, we know, so are kids. We get it. It seemed that the grandmothers had conspired with the minister to make sure that we got the message and that we knew *exactly* what we were getting into with this new little ~~puppy~~ child.

108

Chapter Nineteen: No Place like Home

It was a great day when we finally made it back to Michigan with Anna. Due to the various legal issues involved with interstate adoption and the fact that she was born close to Thanksgiving, the whole process slowed to a virtual crawl. Throw in the fact that November is also National Adoption Month, and you get a whole judicial system clogged with en masse finalizations and other celebrations that put our little situation on the back burner. I ventured back to Jackson a few times after Anna was born to check on the house, get mail, and check in at the college. Tod had not since he was Anna's guardian at the time. We didn't feel comfortable having him out of the state should anything happen. We could go *anywhere* in the state of Ohio with her... all the way down to the West Virginia border, over to the Pennsylvania border, or down to the Kentucky border... we just couldn't cross any state lines with her until the papers cleared in both states.

Our lone trip away from my parents' house was to visit Tod's brother and his wife over the Thanksgiving weekend. Since they also lived in Ohio, we were good to go. Each day we waited in hopes of returning to our home to start our new life with Anna. I will go on record as saying that time stood still for us for those three long weeks. Our families were busy getting ready for the holidays, and we were stuck sitting on the couch watching day time TV and playing with Anna when she was awake. I have never longed to be home so much in my entire life. It was difficult to establish any kind of routine as it wasn't our place. We didn't know how a baby would fit into our home. We had conceptualized it in our minds, but we had no idea.

How will a two story house work with late night bottle feedings?

Will it be warm enough?

Do we have her in the right room?

How will the pets react to her?

About a month after she was born, we both needed to go back to Jackson for the night, and because the adoption wasn't finalized, we couldn't take Anna out of the state. Tod had a professional development workshop he was supposed to attend and was eager for the change. I had to get back to work as it was coming up on finals week. Knowing we would be able to return home soon, we packed my car to the roof and headed north and begrudgingly left her with her new grandparents. We were both nervous as this was the first time we had both been away from her, and the nervousness showed in our voices and our chatter as we headed out of town.

As we passed the city limits of Jackson sign, Tod's phone rang. It was our lawyer. She asked where we were, and we told her that we had pulled into Jackson. She quickly asked if we had the baby, and we assured her that we did not. Sure as shit, not even two minutes after we entered the city without Anna, we were finally cleared to bring her back to Michigan. The paperwork was finally done.

We both cheered and immediately called my folks to have them start packing up Anna for her journey back to Jackson. In retrospect, it was a good thing that we made this trip without her, as the month down in Ohio had generated a lot of stuff for us: dirty clothes, new baby gear, gifts, and other items associated with becoming new parents. I don't think we would have had room for her if we wanted. I had visions of the Joad family heading west from Oklahoma. We weren't Okies looking for work; we were two new dads without a clue.

We pulled into our house, quickly unloaded and excitedly drove back to Ohio. Oscar, Tod's dog, would not leave his side. He followed Tod each time he went to the car and demanded his attention. His behavior was a little needy, but we understood him missing Tod and packed him up in the car for the trip back to my parents' house. Little did he know how his life would change as this new source of fun and never ending food came into his life. When we arrived back in Perrysburg, Oscar ran in, gave my parents' dog Darby a quick sniff and then ran straight to Anna to size her up.

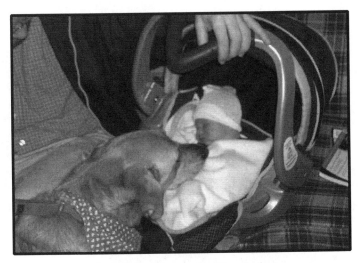

The lab results are in; it's a baby!

We had promised Anna's mom that we would stop by on the way home. I wasn't looking forward to this last goodbye as the day we took Anna home from the hospital was a bleak and depressing day for all involved. What was supposed to be a joyous and happy day for us was filled with tears and sobbing. We called and let them know that we would be stopping by for a brief visit. We picked up our daughter, said a tearful but thankful goodbye to my parents, and headed out to see her mom. The visit went well, as Anna's mom had some of her friends over to meet Anna and her new dads. The sadness that prevailed at the hospital was replaced with joy and happiness as Anna moved into her new home in Michigan. It wasn't a final good-bye but a good-bye for now.

We pulled into Jackson late in the evening. I had imagined a cheerful photo for her baby book with us holding her on our front porch as we went in for the first time as a new family. Instead, under the cover of darkness, we snuck our new little bundle into *our* house. We locked the door and went to bed exhausted but happy. The first few days and weeks back in Jackson were wild. We attempted to retain some sense of normalcy in our lives, but we quickly realized that a new sheriff was in town, and she was calling the shots.

My most vivid memory of those first few days back was the

insanity of us trying to get our Christmas tree in the front door while Anna cried in the background. Our friend from church stopped by and saw us on the porch struggling with the tree. She immediately asked where the baby was and climbed over the tree to go see her, shaking her head and muttering under her breath. I think she was questioning the judge's decision to place this little baby with two complete morons. She took care of Anna for us for a moment, and we began to set up the tree. When I was in college, I worked for Jacobson's Stores as a designer in the Display Department, so I became pretty adept at setting up trees and decorating for the holidays. Not so much anymore. What used to be an afternoon of intense work turned into several weeks of insanity as the big day loomed.

During our time in Ohio, we became very close with Anna's mom and her family and friends, but we desperately wanted to be with *our* friends back home. That first weekend home, we took Anna out for her Jackson debut. We met friends at favorite local restaurants for dinner and a celebration of some kind. I don't remember what we were celebrating, but I do know that Anna stole the show as only babies can do.

We had attended church with Anna's mom in Toledo. We found many similarities to their church and our church at the time. Both were United Methodists, but their church proudly displayed a rainbow pride flag on the altar and had a mostly LGBT congregation in attendance each Sunday. Their church was a fully welcoming and reconciling church, and we were accepted as a new family with open arms. We weren't sure what to expect with our church as it was an older congregation, and we had heard that folks were a little concerned with us adopting. Never mind the fact that we were gay… *Adopting?*

The minister had been taking a lot of crap from some of the membership in the church; a few families left the church when we joined. Some sidebar/coffee-donut conversations that dealt with us and having a kid also transpired. The minister decided to take matters into her own hands and did a proactive strike at the families who were questioning our intentions. She did a weekly kids' message and asked all the little ones to come forward at the beginning of the service for a quick lesson that was an adjunct to what was being preached to the adults. The kids' sermon that day dealt with a variety of subjects regarding families presented in the Bible. The minister shared with the young children on the platform that morning the story of how God sent Jesus to earth but didn't have anyone to take care of him so he asked Joseph to be his father on earth. She, in so many words, spelled out that Jesus, like Anna, had two daddies and a mommy.

That first Sunday at church was a whirlwind of smiling faces, hearty handshakes and hugs. Anna was whisked from our arms the moment we walked in the door and was passed from person to person before the service. We sat in our regular seats in the back of the sanctuary, this time with Anna sleeping on Tod's shoulder. During the announcements, the minister came over to our pew and took Anna from Tod. She walked around with Anna in her arms and passed by each pew, introducing her to the congregation and charging them with her care and upbringing. She drew a line in the sand for us, challenging the congregation to accept and welcome this little girl into their lives without prejudice, living up to the UMC's motto of: Open Doors, Open Hearts, and Open Minds. We'll never know for sure who was against us coming to the church and adopting a child, and at this point, it doesn't matter. What matters is that we were home, physically, spiritually, and emotionally, and in the immortal words of Dorothy Gale, "There's no place like home."

Field Observation:
Broken hand, Broken Hearts (November 2008)

For any of you who were thinking of nominating us for parents of the year, please hold off on your noms please. I am beginning to think that maybe us gays shouldn't adopt after all.

Here's why.

Last week, Anna and I headed to the pet store for Yukon's food. Only one place in town carries the "giant breed" food that he likes. They have little shopping carts in the store, and Anna was being very helpful and pulled one out for me. When she did, the part that houses the child seat and goes up to allow another cart to go in for storage slammed down on her hand. She cried, no *screamed,,* and I pulled her hand up to do a quick triage of the situation.

Through her tears I found out that she could indeed move the fingers, so I immediately ruled out broken bones (per my Red Cross First Aid classes) and worked on calming her down and seeing if there was any blood. She calmed down and we got the food, scoped out some fish and gerbils and were on our way. During check out, she tried to sneak a cookie-shaped dog treat into her mouth and giggled when I told her it would turn her into a dog if she ate it. In my opinion, the cart incident was a memory. Or so we thought. For the next week, she made *no* indication of any kind of injury or pain and played, colored, and even did her tumbling class without any kind of complaining. If you doubt me, please check out the pictures from her birthday post and see if she looks like she's in pain. However...

Last night, Tod was wiping the birthday cake off her hands, and she cried out when he touched her left hand. We checked it out, and her index finger was swollen and a little red. I pointed this out to the daycare lady when I dropped her off this morning and

Jesus Has Two Daddies

she asked her neighbor over (who is a nurse), and she thought we should have it looked at (uh, a week later). So Anna and I headed out to an "express" care here in town. We got there at 9 am and at 1 pm we left with a splint on her now diagnosed hairline fracture. Anna was quite the trooper as Dr. Cubby McHotstuff (he was cute) looked at her hand and sent her off to for x-rays. She even bravely stood at the table and held her hand in position as the creepy x- ray tech barked orders at her from behind her shield. So now, for her big third birthday party on Sunday, we have to find matching ace bandages to go with her outfit as her hand has been splinted to help the finger's healing.

Nice.

We suck.

I called Tod's mom and told her to put the piano that they have (and want to give to us for Anna) up for auction on eBay as Anna's piano career is over for now.

Go ahead, call protective services; we'll talk to them.

Chapter Twenty:
Making it Official

On September 26, 2006, our second-parent adoption for Anna Laura was finalized. We drove north to the courthouse, met both sets of *our* parents, and waited anxiously. Our lawyer was stuck in traffic coming from Ann Arbor.

I took the day off since I knew I wouldn't be able to concentrate. Tod's adoption of Anna was finalized on June 6, 2006 (yes, that was 6/6/06!), but I couldn't adopt until his was legal. We had to wait another three months for my adoption to come up again and to generate more lawyer fees and paperwork. Thankfully, the lawyer that handled Anna's mom's side (at $500 an hour thankyouverymuch) was *not* involved in this process.

Some argued that I had nothing to worry about and that the adoption was a formality. I didn't trust anything. I had heard too much and seen too much, and I was genuinely concerned that something might indeed happen, and I wouldn't be able to be Anna's official parent along with Tod. Our lawyer reassured us that the only thing that could possibly derail the proceedings would be an attack from the Taliban or a meteor crashing through the roof and killing the judge. Tod and I have differing memories of this, so I included both apocalyptic scenarios for your enjoyment. But still, I worried.

The meeting with the judge, a kind older man (hardly the flaming liberal activist judge I expected), was quick and to the point. Tod had to give up custody of Anna to the state for what seemed an eternity, but in actuality it was only a few minutes. My mom said that my neck and then my ears turned bright red as the judge declared Anna a ward of the state. Anna never left our laps, but she was busy trying to move around, oblivious to all the drama unfolding in front of her. After she was turned over to the state, and Tod relinquished all of his rights, the judge declared that Anna was now the proud owner of TWO dads, and that we were both her rightful parents. I have shared this aspect with many parents, and some have laughed and jokingly suggested that they wished that they had the option to relinquish their kids when their kids were being naughty. There has also been talk of the State of Nebraska and their child abandonment law that pretty much made the state a landfill for any unruly or unwanted child. A child craves security; a child craves stability, and a child craves a family.

For a brief moment, Anna had neither. She was officially a ward of the State of Michigan for the few minutes it took the judge to reassign us as legal parents. I can't imagine ever having that happen to me. My worst fear as a kid was that my parents would leave me somewhere and drive off never to be seen again.

*No, I was not sleeping or praying;
I was just listening very intently.*

You could hear a collective sigh from the galley where our parents sat when all was said and done. Hugs and tears abounded as we celebrated a huge milestone. I felt like that character in the chick flick *Waiting to Exhale* as I did just that. That character had held her breath, waiting for that special man; I had held my breath, waiting for that moment when Anna was officially mine. Our family has many milestones to celebrate and remember: birthdays, holidays, anniversaries, but none as important as our Family Day, September

26th. That day, and that heart stopping moment in court will forever be a defining moment in my life. I became a guardian of Anna the day she was born; I became her *Papa* that afternoon in September.

Field Observation:
Where the Wild Things Be (February 2010)

The night Anna wore her dragon suit and made mischief of one kind and another. Her papa called her "WILD THING!" and Anna said "I'LL EAT YOU UP!" so she was sent to bed without eating anything.

It was a gift from a former student, and for a long time, it hung in her play area ignored except for Halloween and when she was bored with her other gowns. Last night, she donned the pink dragon suit and spent much of the night growling and pretending to scratch and claw at the air. While we are happy that she is comfortable being both the princess *and* the dragon during playtime, we were *not* happy with her behavior as the night wore on. We convinced her to change out of the costume, and she did for dinner, but the mentality stuck with her and affected her behavior as we tried to eat. The battles that we face each night with the kids start around 4:30 as they both want a snack and our undivided attention while we are working on transitioning from work and getting dinner ready ourselves. If we stop and play or snuggle, or watch TV with them, then dinner is delayed, and the evening gets longer and longer. But if we don't give them 100%, then the attention grabbing behavior starts. So we try to strike a balance and I have actually become adept at creating meals that can be reheated while I focus on the kids, but that's not always the case.

That night, after a day at home doing errands, Anna's behavior escalated to eleven on the naughty dial. She was out of her routine, and she didn't take a nap, a nasty combination for sure. A few time outs and stern warnings didn't change her behavior at the table, so after outlining the consequences going immediately to her room for the night, she tested us once again.

She should know better. She lives with two teachers.

If you test us, you will fail.

Drama club: Today at noon.

So after the warnings and then some farting around with her green beans, she was whisked upstairs, not passing GO, not collecting $200.

Straight to bed.

And, before you call protective services, she did eat; she didn't finish her meal all the way and definitely had no dessert. But once up in her room, she saw a moment to escape and darted, no, *flew* downstairs to hide. This is the kid who can take 20 minutes to go down the steps in the morning when she doesn't want to do whatever it is we're about to do. She was down in a flash with her 40-something papa in hot pursuit (no really, at this point, I was sweating). This time, I put her on the ground and straddled her, so I could get her pajamas on her. I guess watching all that WWF finally paid off. And, again, before you dial protective services, I was *not* sitting on her. But at this point, she was completely out of control and beyond any kind of reason. I got her dressed and put her into bed and then the screaming started. She loves an audience, but when you leave, she knows that the show is over and reality sets in. I was serious about her going to bed if she continued to act up at the table, and I followed through with it. If I had ignored her, I would have failed her test. While there are some battles to pick, dinner time is not one that we are willing to concede.

So the next morning, I opened her door and woke her up asking if she was going to be my best girl today. She hugged me and said, "Papa... yes!" and then went back under the covers to wait for Eli to come in and wake her up (it's their thing, don't ask). I asked her at breakfast if she was going to be better than she was last night at dinner, and she looked at me with a questioning *whatchootalkin'aboutWillis* face. Apparently, last night was last night, and she was ready to move on, and so was I. It's hard to focus on the fun times with kids when stuff such as this happens, but kids have incredibly short and forgiving memories.

Perhaps we should follow their lead.

122

Chapter Twenty-One:
Life before Kids, a Look Back

THE YEAR BEFORE ANNA was born, Tod and I were ready to head west to Chicago for a weekend of fun and frolic. We had begun the whole adoption process and for the past months, we had been working on "getting ready" (whatever that means) for a new life in our lives. We had told our parents, friends, and coworkers and were busily attending to the myriad of details that go into adoption. In the end, we decided to stay home in Jackson for the long weekend instead of cavorting with our friends in the Windy City. We ended up nesting pretty much the entire three days, doing what we thought we should be doing to get our house and lives ready for this yet unknown little one. We cleaned and organized the house, purging ourselves of a lot of shit… both physical and mental. We told ourselves that if we did have a kid we'd still be able to do all of the wild and fascinating things we did as D.I.N.K.s (Double Income No Kids) and maintain our absolutely fabulous lifestyle. Our recent trip to NYC had us walking the streets of the metropolis evaluating what we could and couldn't do with a kid. Central Park, yes, The Eagle, NO.

This was both a resignation to the fact that we were becoming parents and the realization that life didn't end if we didn't go to Chicago. I think we actually felt better by not going and pooling our efforts and energy into getting ready for our future child and the home study later. The home study is perhaps the most grueling part of the adoption process. Your entire life is evaluated and picked over to see if you are worthy. We had no idea what to expect, so this time helped ease these fears.

I distinctly remember getting ready to go away for the weekend before the kids came. We had made plans to head north to visit Traverse City and relax. I stopped by the store for some provisions on my way home from work the day we left. My hastily scribbled grocery list had the following:

Beer
Wine
Tequila
Cat food

Apparently, I had somehow managed to pick up Amy Winehouse's grocery list by mistake. The only thing missing was heroin. Those halcyon weekends of idle chit chat, reading magazines, and staring at the lake are gone. It's a cold hard fact: life with a kid is much different.

We had talked about this prior to the adoption, and we were okay with the stuff we might be giving up to start our family. I must say that my days of thumbing magazines are pretty much gone for now. I used to subscribe to the likes of *Gourmet*, *Food and Wine*, *Spin*, and a whole host of other "lifestyle" magazines. This was way before reality hit and made me realize that Rachael Ray may be the Messiah. I recently went through my recipes, a somewhat organized collection of clippings and whatnot from the many years of pre-child epicurean journals. I tossed most of the recipes for kindling in the fireplace and stuck with what worked. I kept the dinners that got me out of the kitchen in less than 30 minutes and didn't require a trip to Trader Joes, Whole Foods, or sneaking on to the set of *Iron Chef* to steal that week's secret ingredient.

Now that I am a parent, my thumbing material is now *Family Fun*, *Parents*, and *Adoptive Families*. My only hold out from my pre-Anna days is *Entertainment Weekly*. You can have that subscription when you pry it out of my cold, dead, hands. Thankfully, the aforementioned journals are easily read during my morning constitutional and don't require much thought or time commitment. I can keep up with what's cool and happening even though I spend more time with *iCarly* and *Yo Gabba Gabba* and not the cool kids in *Spin* and *Rolling Stone*. I also used to love shopping. It was fun to leisurely stroll through our local mall or head to Ann Arbor for an afternoon of gallery hopping or window shopping. That's all changed. Now I am ninja-like in my ability to get in and get out without having to hit the toy aisle and without having to buy up the candy by the cash register to keep the kids quiet. Yes, there are days when I can get out and do my thing and look at art, but most days require picking up milk or bread, not art or wine. Yes, there is still wine on our list, it's spelled WHINE.

Anna's picture of her family. The girl needs some classes on how to use a camera.

Field Observation:
What is a Family? (December 2007))

I was putting up the Christmas tree in our attic family room one year, and Anna was busy playing and half watching *Cailou* (the preschool television show). Anna and I have the ability to be in the room and do our separate things without being in each other's space, even back then. We play a Marco Polo of sorts; it's our version of sonar, and it helps me keep in touch with her without being obtrusive. So as we pinged our comments back and forth to each other, we both carried on with the tasks at hand.

    Me: Hey look, it's one of Papa's former student's ornaments; isn't it pretty?
    Anna: Cailou is playing outside now.

Me: Do you like Bugs Bunny?
Anna: Cailou has a coat on.
Me: Look, it's Tinky Winky!
Anna: Cailou has a Mommy.
Great silence in the room. I go about my business.
Anna: Cailou has a Daddy.
More crickets chirping; I break out in a cold sweat.
Anna: Cailou has a Mommy and Daddy.

I put down the Yukon Cornelius ornament that I was about to hang up and gathered my thoughts. I calmly asked, "What does Anna have?" She responded as only a two year old can: "Anna has Daddy and Papa."

For a young child, she has an amazing grasp on her life and her family structure. I hope this holds until she is older.

Chapter Twenty-Two:
Bridge? Intermission? Snack Time?

Even though I am now not attending church, the goings on associated with the church still hold great interest to me and what I teach at the college in art history. Without the church, most art history classes would be boring. Growing up Protestant, our little Congregational church was a hideous wooden box with bad lighting. I envied my Catholic friends who went to services in soaring cathedrals or ornately decorated chapels in town with amazing artwork, stained glass, incense and old pipe organs. When I went through Confirmation classes, I hung on every word that the teacher said and began to study. Suddenly, all the things that were going on in front of me each Sunday made sense. I had long since taken my First Communion, but it wasn't until Confirmation, that I understood that some religions actually thought it was Christ in the bread and wine. I also became aware of the church's liturgical calendar. I had noticed that the paraments went from white to red to purple to green throughout the year. My naïve assumption was that someone changed them and put up what colors they liked. I had no idea that the colors were associated with the various "seasons" of the church and changed throughout the year. As a side note, I scored a perfect 100% on my Confirmation test, beating out the instructor's daughter, who actually failed the test. So yeah, I am the religious right's worst nightmare, a homo who knows the Bible.

So why all this?

The time between the tongue wagging of Pentecost and the candle lighting of Advent is a pretty boring time in the church year. It is known as Ordinary Time as not much happens during this time. I would guess that after Anna's adoption was finalized, we too went into our own little version of Ordinary Time.

Yes, there were milestones that were reached, and yes, they were exciting and precious and are forever burned into our memories.

However, they will bore you to death should I start writing about them in detail. The annoying thing about new parents is they think that their baby is the *only one* to ever do anything in that oh-so-precious, very-special way. Yes, we were those parents, and not only did we take pictures, but we blogged about it.

I hate us.

An event worth mentioning here are the post-placement checkups by the Adoption Agency. We had two after Anna came to live with us, ironically, neither of them at our house. These were necessary to complete the paperwork toward Tod's adoption of Anna. The first one was done in the conference room of the agency, and Anna cooed and played in her car seat while the social worker talked with us about how things were going with our new child. The second one was not so smooth. The social worker could not get into the building as it was the weekend. It was also the middle of winter, and it was nasty cold. Sitting outside was not an option, so the four of us sat in our car in the parking lot while the social worker asked her questions and filled out the necessary paperwork.

After our second-parent adoption was finalized, we were pretty much your average homo couple raising a kid in one of the alleged birthplaces of the Republican Party.

Nothing to see here, move along.

Anna's addition to our family brought some big and some not so big changes to our lives. Most notably, we became total homebodies, even to the point of redoing our spacious third floor attic to create a man-kid cave to hole up in. I was sick of toys in every room of the house, so we worked with a local contractor to expel the bats and transform the space into our new favorite place to hang out. There are spots for the kids to play, a swing to swing on, and all the goodies you could want for your entertainment. We purposely didn't put a bathroom up there because we knew if we did, we'd never leave the space. So with our new kid and new fort three stories up in the air, we settled into parenting a toddler.

We didn't go out, and when we did, we were too tired to do anything fun. We took a road trip to Columbus to party with our friends (after securing Anna with my parents) and the first night down there, we were in the hotel room sleeping soundly by 9:00. There was no Scarlet A for us; it was the Scarlet L, for LAME. While our friends slowly emerged for breakfast the next day hung over and groggy, we were chipper and ready to go after a much needed night's sleep without the midnight feedings, diaper changes, or calls from down the hall.

Anna progressed along the merry path of infant to toddler in a pretty normal fashion. We somehow managed to dodge the dreaded terrible twos, and got the WTF fours instead.

Seriously, she was a happy, cheerful kid, a kid who always seemed to have a smile on her face. But once four hit, all bets were off. The screaming went to hysterical levels and the "IHATEYOUIWISHYOUWEREDEAD!" that I anticipated around age 16 was suddenly in my face on a somewhat regular basis.

My request for a sabbatical from the college was approved for winter semester 2009. From January to May, I was released from my duties at the college and spent much of that winter up in the attic working on personal projects, as well as a project for the college regarding art history. It was fun to be able to take a day and hang out with my kid. We got on all the mailing lists for toddler/preschool happenings and spent that cold winter playing, reading, singing, and enjoying each other's company. Anna, our dear friend Deborah, and I even took a trip to Detroit's Heidelberg Project one wickedly cold February morning. After exploring that colorful and artistic enclave, we hit Greektown and the Detroit Art Institute, stopping to warm up with hot cocoa and cookies along the way. It was blissful. We took several other big trips that year, including the big one to New York City for Tod's spring break. It was nice that Anna was finally portable. She rarely needed a diaper, and the days of leaving the house looking like you were headed out for a mountain-climbing expedition were done.

This "in between time" had several milestones aside from the walking, talking, pooping on the toilet events that should be shared. Anna's mom called us out of the blue one day and told us that she was pregnant again. We were a bit surprised for several reasons:

1. She was now a full-time college student and loving it.
2. She had a difficult delivery, so they weren't sure she would be able to get pregnant without medical intervention.

They asked us to meet them in Chelsea, MI for dinner, so we could talk. Immediately we started thinking that she would ask us to raise this child as well. We headed out that day with feelings of excitement and anticipation. As we settled in at the table and Anna and her mom played, we started talking about details. The boyfriend was the father, and she was a few months into the pregnancy. There were a few beats of idle chit chat about how it was going as we looked at the menu and ordered.

Finally, I broke.

I asked if they were going to parent this child, and they both responded yes. So this child would be Anna's half-sister, living an hour and a half away with her mom. We talked to Anna about this on the way home and did our best to explain to her the situation. We shared with Anna the fact that her Mommy was now older and a "big girl" and not the 15-year-old we met several years earlier. We talked about how when you grow up and get older, you can do more things and have more responsibilities. She nodded in her car seat and seemed to comprehend the situation better than we could have imagined. She was thrilled to have a sibling on the way, and as the pregnancy progressed, we found out that it would be another girl, so Anna would now be the big sister, albeit, a sister at a distance.

We also went to California in August of 2008 and were legally married on the seventh anniversary of our original commitment ceremony in 2001. We were married by an international DJ (Jeb Edwards, Google him) on the 4th floor of San Francisco's glorious City Hall, not too far from the watchful gaze of Harvey Milk's memorial bust. Jeb's husband Thomas wrangled Anna and her cousin Cole before the ceremony took place and managed to keep them both from sliding down the huge marble banister to the first floor. We didn't have a Bridezilla on our hands; we had a perky flower-girl/ring-bearer that didn't seem to be affected at all by jet lag and was doing her best to test Thomas' patience.

Jesus Has Two Daddies

♦ ♦ ♦

We also worked hard, *really* hard, to get Obama elected and spent much of that election cycle working for the campaign. We were able to score VIP entrance to an event in Battle Creek, MI and were less than fifty feet from him and Joe Biden as they addressed the enthusiastic crowd. Anna was with us and happily played on the turf as we waited for Obama's appearance later that night. She was still in diapers at the time and needed a change. So there in front of the gathered thousands, Anna was naked from the waist down for a brief bit at an Obama rally. I wish I could say the same about myself. It was blazingly hot that day.

And then, flash forward to Mothers' Day, 2009.

Many kingdoms and regimes have crumbled or dissolved in my time, some to great fanfare, some very benignly. None, however, would have as great an impact on me as the dissolving of Anna's tiny little kingdom where she was the P.I.C., the Princess In Charge. That Mothers' Day was the call to arms, and soon, a tiny, but vocal Prince would be in Anna's life, challenging her rule as the P.I.C.

Field Observation:
Anna Sends a Memo (March 2009)

The poorly named *Parents* Magazine had a full page article called *Memo to Mommy*.

We got a free subscription when Anna was born, and we stuck with it because it was cheap, and every so often, they provide some good information or recipes. The magazine is otherwise a joke as it tends to focus on MOMS only... men are dragged out in June for Fathers' Day and then tucked away for the rest of the year. One issue had full-bodied pictures of the moms, but the dads were actually headless in the photo shoot. The magazine should be renamed *Female Parent*, and not *Parents*.

The editorial board apparently thinks that it is okay to

present dads as an absent class in their articles and photos. An article by Mary Mohler in the September 2008 issue hung on our fridge with Mommy crossed out and Daddy & Papa scribbled in over the gyno-focused title. Mohler's article offered a few chestnuts of wisdom, much of what we already knew.

But some of them took some readjustment:

1. *Stop freaking out about the mess!*

I tend to be a pretty neat person and have a manic dislike for clutter. As I type, I am sitting in the attic family room surrounded by the three days' worth of playtime with Anna. Puzzle pieces and doll clothes are tossed about as well as several other ankle breaking toys. I have learned to sigh, shake my head, and walk on.

2. *Let me do it!*

I read this, and a mental image of the character Stuart from *Mad TV* popped up in my head. Sure, it's easy to try and enforce, but when you're trying to get out the door in the morning, sometimes you have to do it yourself. When you calm down and realize that much of a toddler's life is a teachable moment, you have to let them do their will even if it means you'll be late.

3. *Don't let me think you're perfect*

Uh, that's an easy one Mary, please. If a kid has eyes, they will know that their parents are far from perfect. We need to remember that we are *always* on stage and being studied intently by our little charge.

4. *Love me, even when I am naughty. I will only be this age once.*

It seems that just a few moments ago, I woke up and was a father. Now I am enrolling her in preschool and fretting about how to pay for her schooling. I have to shake my head each day as she grows and grows and is quickly becoming a young girl headed toward school.

5. *Keep your promises. It's about trust. When I am a teenager, you'll understand why it is important.*

Everything Tod and I say to Anna is a promise. She will hear much in her life, but the words from a parent are always the words that mean the most especially when the child is her age. Tod and I endeavor to keep our promises, but sometimes we say things just to get out the door. As our daycare provider states, "Whatever it takes!" is sometimes the route to go when your kid wants to wear their Princess outfit to the store, or is refusing to put on their boots, etc.

I will always stand behind my words, but sometimes life gets in the way.

"Can we go to the park today?" "Oh sure honey... after work." But then the day goes south, plans get derailed, and the last thing you want to do is go to a park. So how do you break a promise?

It's not easy.

But one promise I made and I take very seriously. Some people are parents by accident; others, such as Tod and me, had to go quite far to make parenthood a reality. I will always be Anna Laura's parent as I promised the court. I will always do my best to work to that end and provide for her the best I can. I will be there to listen; I will be there to play; I will be there to talk; I will be there to read stories; I will be there to hold her hand when she's scared; I will be there to kiss her goodnight, and most of all, I will be the bestest Papa she ever has.

Promises are for keeping.

PART TWO

Chapter Twenty-Three: Eli's Coming

> *Eli's comin'*
> *Eli's comin' (Eli's a-comin')*
> *Well you better hide your heart, your loving heart*
> *Eli's a-comin' and the cards say... a broken heart*
>
> Three Dog Night, *Eli's Coming*.

Objects in the rearview mirror are crankier than they appear

On Mothers' Day 2009, our minister stopped us prior to church and mentioned that her friend, a social worker, was trying to place a boy with a same-sex couple.

Were we interested?

She didn't know much, but she knew that bonding would be an issue, since this boy had been in foster care for much of his life.

We knew that since we were "off" as teachers during the summer, we might be a good match. We told her to contact her friend and tell her we'd be interested. In the meantime, Tod's parents were coming over for the holiday, and we had food to get ready while we assembled our home-study papers and birth parent letter under the cloak of secrecy.

Our minister told us that her friend was a no-nonsense kind of person, so if she began talking to us after reading our information, we could pretty much guarantee that she had picked us for placement.

We faxed our stuff to her and waited.

We went through the week not knowing what to do. Our minister talked with the social worker, who said that we could create a book for the boy in anticipation of the transition from foster care to placement with us. We combed our many picture files and made a collection of photos showing who we were as a family for his photo album. I remembered my Children's Literature class, and printed out a simple, repetitive text for the photos. "Anna, Daddy, and Papa" started each picture heading. The pictures showed us playing, during the holidays, or at the pool swimming. Having this little task seemed to keep us from going crazy with anticipation and uncertainty.

Due to a variety of circumstances, the social worker was extremely overworked, so it came as no surprise that the initial phone call from her came on a late Friday afternoon. I had carried my cell phone and the landline wherever I went that week in anticipation of her call. As it would happen, she called when I was in the shower and Tod was gone to get the babysitter for our date night that night. Tod heard the phone ringing as he closed the door to leave, but assumed that I would answer it. I listened to her message, and I quickly called her back on her cell phone, even though she said she would "get with us next week." We talked for quite a bit, setting up a meeting for the following Tuesday. I kept my phone conversation quiet as we settled Anna with the sitter and headed out to find food prior to the cabaret performance. When our beers came, I told Tod about the conversation, and we offered a toast to our potential new son. Reality set in as we waited for our food.

We had talked with the minister during the week as she was eager to find out what we knew. She and her partner are adoptive

Jesus Has Two Daddies

parents as well, with two little girls. She was in contact with the social worker and would relay our thoughts and messages to her as we waited for her to contact us. A while back, we stopped at the park across from our church, and Anna tossed a penny into the fountain to make a wish. We asked her what she wished for and she said, "A little brother!" The pastor shared this with the social worker, and she remarked that she couldn't compete with that kind of cuteness.

As the meeting with the social worker came closer, we puttered around the house getting stuff ready for the boy to come live with us. During our initial home study for Anna, I cleaned as if I had never cleaned before. Our house was spotless and everything was in its place. For this meeting, my level of concern was high for sure, but now that we are parents, my sense of reality took precedence over the need to clean. If we presented a house that housed a three-year-old, a 150 pound St. Bernard, and was too clean, she'd think we were freaks. I cleaned up the chunks of food and called it good as I quickly stashed stuff in closets and vacuumed up the visible crumbs and clumps of dog hair.

The meeting went well. We were all in a pretty good space when she came and were sitting in the living room calmly reading when the doorbell rang. We sat around our dining room table and began to talk about life, kids, adoption, and this little guy who was the center of our attention. We talked about the boy's history, and I kept asking questions as we had made a list at lunch of things we thought we should know. As his narrative was read to us off his file, our questions were answered and we began to know more about who this little guy was. His birth parents were drug users, and he tested positive for marijuana at birth. His weight was normal and his Apgar score was 9 (which is good). We found out that his name was Elija, and we debated keeping his name since his birth parents live here in Jackson. We settled on keeping the name and calling him Eli for short but added an H at the end for a more Biblical appropriate Elijah.

I tend to be the one that errs on the side of caution and will believe it when I see it. As the social worker shared more and more about Eli, I stopped the conversation and asked point blank if this was a match for placement. She said yes and the news began to sink in for good. Instead of using speculative language, we began to talk in terms of this happening for sure within the next few months.

I asked if we could see pictures, but she said that people tend to get stupid and stop listening once they see the pictures. She wanted to finish up the paperwork before we could see him. When that time came, my hands were sweaty, and my heart was beating fast. I got up to get Anna a snack as the social worker pulled out the pictures from his file. It was a collection of studio shots from the studio at the mall. I came back to the table with pictures of my future son spread out for us to see for the first time. Being in the delivery room when Anna was born gave me a front row seat for the birth process and showed me more than any health class movie ever could. I wasn't sure what to expect because I was worried about what he might look like due to the drug issue and some other health issues (now resolved) that were visible on his body. What I saw was a young boy with a smile that could light up a room. He has blonde hair, so of course he looks bald in all the photos, but he had bright eyes and a killer smile.

The social worker called Anna over and asked her if she wanted to see her little brother. Anna pored over the pictures and after a moment pointed at one and said, "I like that one!"

We agreed.

Fate dealt him a crappy hand at birth, but we were about to change that and offer him a loving home forever.

The first meeting with Eli and Anna went well. It was the perfect Fathers' Day for us. Anna was a bit off the week before, as she knew what was going on. Her behavior bordered on crazed at times. I contemplated calling the neighbors to let them know that we were *not* beating her. The screaming reached epic proportions. Her behavior, which can be oppositional, went to downright naughty. We had a discussion with one of our friends, and he remarked "Well, she IS a princess you know." I think she realized that her monarchy was crumbling as there was a prince coming in to help her rule.

We arrived at the foster parents' home and all was well. Anna was happy to meet her new brother (who was now over a year old) and charmed the foster parents with her insane cuteness. The foster mom had gone out and bought us Fathers' Day cards. Apparently she

Jesus Has Two Daddies

searched three or four different stores to find a papa card for me and couldn't locate one. I was incredibly touched by this gesture.

We played, we talked, and we watched the two new siblings get to know each other. Sharing is not a new concept for Anna as she has to share at day care. But this was meeting Eli on his turf, and he had all the goods. We had a big blue Ikea bag full of her old toys set aside for Eli for when he came to live with us, but Anna started dipping in to the bag to reclaim ownership of her toys. After a quick dinner and pleasantries, we headed back to Jackson leaving Eli with the foster parents. The day after was pretty mellow, and we spent much of the day at the pool swimming and hanging out in the sun. Apparently Eli was wiped out, as we got this note from his foster Mom:

Eli was definitely a whipped puppy! After you guys left I offered him a bottle (even though he hadn't had one in three days, I'm bad!!). I thought it would sooth him and settle him down, so he could sleep well. You know how you sleep when you're over tired. He drank about an ounce and lapsed into a coma! I had to wake him up to get him ready for the doctor's appointment, and that wasn't until 10:30! He took a four hour nap then a two hour nap around supper time. Then to bed at 8:45! HAHAHA

As the early summer wore on, the visits got longer and Elijah was getting into the rhythm of life with us and his new big sister. The baby gates went back up, and we had his room set up and stocked with diapers and wipes and some of the goodies we saved from Anna's early years. Anna's first pair of black Chuck Taylor's hung next to my desk after she outgrew them. Now they are back in the drawer in Eli's room ready for that first hipster dad and son moment.

It came rather quickly, and I will admit that I wasn't ready for the change. We had been told that this would take a while, and we were estimating that it would be some time in August. But as we were packing up the car to go camping, we got a call from the social worker asking us to come to Lansing to sign some papers for consent/ placement the following week.

HOLY SHIT!

We threw everything in the car and headed north instead of west to camp. Anna and I sat in the parking lot of the agency and listened to music while Tod went in and signed for Elijah's placement. We hadn't talked about when he would come. A definite benefit to adoption is that you can often pick when you child will arrive. "Um, Tuesday's just not good for us, can we make it Wednesday?"

We had some idea as to when the transition was to take place, either the following Tuesday or Wednesday, but we needed to finalize with the foster family to make sure. My mind whirled as we headed west to drop Anna off at Tod's parents' house and then head off to camp. I wanted to be home when Elijah came to stay with us, but since this was spring semester and I was teaching, I needed to make plans to accommodate my schedule. I wasn't going to pass out cigars or anything, but I felt that this was a pretty important milestone in his little life. Thankfully, he has had stability with his foster family, but I wanted to be there to present a strong face and strong family when he was "delivered" to our house for the first time.

I asked the foster mom if we needed to come up to get him, and she said, "No, I like to deliver my kids. They've had a rough start, and I want them to know that I didn't just disappear, but I brought them to their new home to start anew." The couple that offered Eli foster care is beyond amazing, and we are blessed to have them as part of Eli's life. In the past, the present, and (we hope), in the future.

Their refrigerator is covered with pictures of foster kids through the years. Class pictures, sports pictures, prom pictures, they're all there. A whole host of kids from all walks of life have transitioned with them over the years, more than forty children in all they estimate.

So on a muggy Wednesday morning in July, they showed up with Eli and a few shopping bags full of clothes, books, and toys. He lit up when he saw us and immediately grabbed for Tod. I could see that his foster mom was fragile with her emotions, so I offered coffee and some donuts. She said no and that they had to get going. We snapped a few pictures and then the good-byes started. Anna and I had picked up a gift for them earlier that morning as a small token of our appreciation for all they had done. I slipped the gift and a note into her hand and warned her that it was a pretty emotional note, so they might want to wait. She wiped her eyes and agreed.

Here's a little snippet from the letter:

Words can't describe our feelings today; it's a day much like the day we brought Anna home from the hospital in Toledo. With our joy comes some pain, and we can't move on without acknowledging that. The day we stepped out of the lobby at St. Ann's Hospital was a day we will never forget. A day wrapped in the joy of the family that we were about to start, and the sorrow of a young girl who was unable to raise the child she gave birth. We are forever in your debt for getting Elijah off to a great start in his young life and will continue to nurture the relationship you all have with this great kid. We know that the past few months have been an exciting and emotional rollercoaster for us all, and we are glad to have worked with a couple so dedicated and concerned about the well-being of these kids.

You two are an amazing couple and do a job that is much needed in this crazy world of ours. We are honored to have you in our lives and are blessed knowing that Eli had you when he needed you most.

We all got a little teary as they said their final goodbyes to Eli, but as we waved to them driving away, a sense of happiness came over the house. We were parents again. We weren't in a delivery room; we weren't at a hospital exhausted from sleeping on waiting room chairs. We were on our front porch and somewhat tan, rested, and ready to go. I can regale folks with my tales of Anna's birth and how I cut the cord and helped coach her birth mom during the delivery, but I can also talk about how nice it was to have Eli join our home on a muggy July morning, delivered not by a doctor or midwife, but by two of the nicest people you'll ever meet.

Field Observation:
You Ruined My Life! (July 2009)

I had a taste of my future one day when this event took place (thanks to Tod for his journaling of this episode):

Anna: I've got to go potty.

Tom: Okay, go and come right back.

[Bells hanging on door handle ring as front door is opened]

Tom: Where did Anna just go?

Tod: Apparently out on the front porch.

[Tom running to front door]

Tom: Anna, why did you just pee on the front porch? That was very naughty, you are in time out.

[Five minutes later while feeding Anna dinner]

Tom: Why did you go out on the front porch to pee?

Anna: [Arms crossed in front of her chest] Because I'm mad at you.

Tom: Why are you mad at me?

Anna: Because you ruined my life!

Tom and Tod: [Hysterical laughing, unable to talk]

And… scene.

Oh sure, laugh now bitches, but apparently the daycare lady is letting the kids watch Maury and Jerry instead of Sprout or PBS. *I ruined her life?*

Really?

Two days before I took Anna and her BFF Chloe to Cedar Point for a day of rides and sugar. The next day we hung out and enjoyed life as we do here on Greenwood. I got my comeuppance a few days later when she had a giant sucker that she won at the Toy House at their 50th birthday party out on the front porch. I suggested that she eat the massive sweet from a bowl, but she opened the confection and headed out to the front porch without heeding my suggestion and promptly dropped the sucker on the porch, shattering it into a dozen pieces. She began to pick up the pieces as I handed her the bowl that I hid behind my back when I came out. She looked up and asked, "Papa, can I eat these?" I looked her right in the eyes and asked, "I don't know, has anyone peed on the porch lately?" She gave me her best three-going-on-four "Bitch, please" look and stuck a chunk of sucker in her mouth.

We are in so much trouble.

CHAPTER TWENTY-FOUR:
HIDE YOUR HEART, HIDE YOUR TOYS

As THE SUMMER MOVED on, we got wrapped up in our own routines with school, work, and daycare, and life seemed to be settling into a delightfully predictable grind. I went back to work full time mid-August, but we did not have daycare, so that left Tod with two kids who were still getting to know each other. This tested the limits of our patience and that made for some stressful days. I took advantage of my Dean's offer for FMLA time off and missed two of the Professional Development days offered the week before classes started. It was nice to have that down time to do nothing. No really, we did *nothing* one whole day. We sat on our butts and watched T.V. It was magical.

As timid as he may have been around Anna at first, Eli quickly became much bolder around her. He initially took whatever she did to him, stealing his toys, hitting him, or biting him. He's much more active in his reaction to these offenses, and there have been moments where we have had to bite our tongues, so we didn't LOL at the situation before us. A perfect example took place at Tod's parents' house. Anna was playing with some Legos, and Eli had two of them that were *across the room* from her. She spied them in his hands and rushed over to grab them from him telling him, "NO ELI! I was playing with them, they're MINE!"

Remember the seagulls from *Finding Nemo*?

MINE! MINE! MINE! MINE! MINE! MINE! MINE! MINE!

Eli went about his business and found some other blocks and put together a pretty sizeable stack. He then came up behind Anna and smashed the blocks over her head like a wrestler would do with a folding chair over his opponent's head. He squealed with glee as he brought down the blocks to her head and then ran off. Anna then stood up screaming and crying in "pain." There probably was some pain involved, but I am certain that it wasn't just her head that was hurting but also her pride. I had to look away as she put on the act of her young life and feigned outrage over his behavior. The pressure in my head from stifling the laugh about caused a hemorrhage in my skull.

There will be tears.

Field Observation:
Careful What You Wish For (January 2010)

It was all fine and dandy when she was being cute and tossing coins in the fountain across from our church each Sunday. The melt-your-heart "I want a little brother!" wishes were enough to choke up anyone with a working soul. We let her do the wishing and kept to ourselves the plans unfolding for Eli to come and live with us. Once we knew it was going to happen, we told her, and she was thrilled and eagerly helped us get ready for his arrival. Oh sure, there were rough moments (such as the "you've ruined my life" outburst), but for the most part, the transition has been pretty smooth.

Christmas break proved a little stressful for all of us, Anna included. The stress of the preschool Christmas Party circuit took its toll (which began mid-December by the way) as did Anna's desire to be on Santa's good little girls list. She did her damnedest to be good, but each day it became harder and harder. We decided that at about 5:00 pm or so, she simply ran out of good. She also completely won me over with her exclaiming one night that "Plankton was in my brain!" There is an episode of *SpongeBob* where Plankton gets in SpongeBob's head and takes control of his body and brings havoc to Bikini Bottom. It's hard for me to get mad at her when she drops a great excuse like that, especially such a great pop culture reference such as SpongeBob.

Add a helping of sugar, an insane holiday travel schedule, no day care or preschool, and you have a recipe for a Category Five Preschool Meltdown. It happened last week, right before the New Year. Cabin fever set in, as did holiday fatigue. Little things caused big problems. If you've ever watched VH1's *Behind the Music*, there is usually a moment in the show when the narrator says, "And then things began to fall apart." Well, if we had a narrator, those words would have been uttered for us as well. The screaming, the yelling, the throwing of things and general bad behavior made for one stressful night here on Greenwood. Thankfully, it was winter, so our doors and windows were closed, and no one could hear the symphony of chaos coming from our kitchen. I don't remember what triggered it, but it happened. Eli did it; Anna reacted; Anna got the time out, and the screaming began.

"I don't want a little brother anymore!"

As the older sibling, I can relate to her feelings. The younger kid is usually nothing but trouble and pretty much ruins the idyllic setup you have with your parents as the only child. Oh sure, we talked about this and warned her that she would have to share her toys, her house, her daddy and papa, but that warning seemed to have been forgotten when the above screamed at the top of her lungs. I looked at her and said that I felt her pain, and that little brothers were annoying. We both laughed a bit, and I calmly told her that we could not return Eli as we forgot to get a receipt.

If they ever record a CD, this is totally going to be on their album cover.

Tod, the second child in his family, got a bit defensive (I believe he punched me) as Anna and I bonded over this issue and curtly he pointed out that this same meltdown probably took place with me and with his older brother when we became big brothers. I doubt it. His brother and I are totally rational beings; we'd never do anything like this.

When the process began with Eli, we had hoped his adoption would be finalized by Christmas, but the six month wait period ends in January instead of December. Our social worker asked to have it pushed up to December, but we were asked to wait. We're okay with that, as some of the best gifts of the holiday season are the ones you get after the mad rush. The ones you can take your time with and enjoy without all the insanity of the holidays.

Chapter Twenty-Five:
Missin My Kids

WE WERE PICKED BY Anna's mom to raise her for a variety of reasons discussed earlier in the book. We have an open adoption, and we see Anna's mom and her family (including Anna's sister) on a regular basis. We use Facebook and share pictures through Flickr, so our relationship is both cyber and real. Anna is okay with that even asking if we are going to Skype with the Grandparents or get in front of the computer to record a message to send her mom or sister. So our open adoption is pretty transparent on all accounts. We do not know who Anna's biological father is, and we will probably never know. With Eli, the situation is much different. Eli was taken away from his birthparents because they weren't taking care of him and he became ill under their (non)care. Thankfully, a young family member realized something was horribly wrong with him and took him to the hospital, which is where the state stepped in and removed him from his parents' care. I had a chance to read Eli's file, a thick book full of both the good and the bad. The first few months of his life were the bad part, but once the little guy got well, things began to improve thanks to the remarkable care he received in foster care. I took a paper and pen to the meeting with the social worker at the beginning stages of the adoption as I wanted to find out as much as I could about him. APGAR scores and other key birth factors were a mystery to us (but not my Mom, a retired OB/GYN nurse, who encouraged me to get what information I could), but as I pored through his records, I stumbled on his birth-parents' names. I was going to quickly write them down, but the social worker saw what page I was on and chimed in, "Oh, that's so-and-so's deposition, and here you'll find so-and-so's court record." What I thought was to be secret was suddenly out in the open. The social worker saw me scribbling notes and asked if I wanted a copy of all this. "Sure," I responded, not knowing if I was even allowed to view these rather disturbing documents. Within a few moments, I was able to know more about Eli and his family than I ever wanted to know. The social worker remarked that I needed to know all this, so I could understand where my future son had come from. Eli's adoption was final, and questions were coming up. The social worker asked us for a recent picture as Eli's father had requested one. We didn't have to comply, but we did. She also asked us about what kind of relationship, if any, we wanted to have with his birth parents. We knew when we first started the process that an open adoption was what we wanted, but we had no idea that this kind of situation would ever exist. His parents didn't have a choice; he was taken away from them to ensure his health and safety. This was a criminal case, cut and dried. We had many discussions about this, together and with the former foster mom. She reports that neither parent is a threat, but she reminded us that when they abused and neglected their son, they lost all rights to him. I did what many of our adoptive family friends have done, and call it unethical or plain nosey, but I looked up Eli's birth parents on Facebook. Since his bio-dad is rather transient, he doesn't have an account; however, his bio-mom is settled and has an account. I didn't friend her, don't worry, but I did find out that we have some friends in common from my years teaching. I scanned through her account and found wall postings like this:

- Juzt Got Out Of Jail...Mizz'N My Kidz!
- Mizz'N Hym! Wish'N I Could Tell Hym How I Really Feel!
- Shit Is Not Goin Rite...I Still Love Hym And Alwayz Will.. Need To Write Hym...Need To Find Out How He Is Doing! I Mizz The Way He Could Brighten My Day...It's Almost Been 1 Year!
- Thank God Christmas Is Over! I hated It! Mizz'n My Babiez! Wish'N I Could Tell Him How I Really Feel... {So Confused)

Field Observation:
A Letter from Papa (June 2010)

One afternoon, I noticed a lady glaring at us as we moved through Target. Anna was having a *horrible afternoon,* and her howls and complaints could be heard through the store. I wrote this letter to the unidentified spinster and suddenly, life was good again.

> *Dear Lady,*
>
> *Thank you so much for your judgmental looks at both me and my daughter yesterday afternoon. Your stink eye looks and sneers as Anna was having her age-appropriate meltdown really helped the situation. Between the staggering heat, not sleeping well, and going through her last day of school, Anna was a perfect storm of emotions and bad behavior as we checked out. Yes, I saw you as we were walking through the store, and I saw your little sneers as Anna demanded toys and other goodies in the toy department. I also noticed that you didn't have a wedding ring on, which probably means you are not married and do not have children of your own. I bet your precious Mr. Whiskers is just a purr-fectly behaved kitty and does exactly what you tell him to do each and every day. Good for you. Go get a lint roller; you have cat hair on your ass.*
>
> *I also noticed that you had single serving food items, which supports my theory that you do indeed live alone and are probably a hateful bitch. I appreciate you not saying anything as I would have had to have a little side bar conversation with you should you have decided to open your trap and comment on her behavior. I appreciated the "hang in there" from the lady in the toy department as she saw my exasperation with Anna, and I really appreciate the checkout guy engaging Eli while Anna moved up to Category 5 on the meltdown scale. Those little gestures were appreciated and kept me from having a full-on stroke at the checkout.*

Yes, we know, kids should be seen and not heard, but that doesn't always happen. I am sorry that your trip out for dinner after an action packed afternoon of cat grooming and watching your stories was interrupted by a little girl with some big things on her plate. She may look mature and sound mature, but in reality, she's a five-year-old, a little girl who is working on being able to control her emotions and behavior. I was able to remain calm while dealing with this situation thanks to those two offering their support while all this was happening. Your tacit disapproval did nothing for the situation but did indeed put you in the running for Bitch of the Year. Go back to your apartment. Mr. Whiskers misses you.

 Sincerely,

 Papa Tom

Author's Note: I posted this on my Facebook page as I felt it needed to be shared with a larger audience. As the comments came in, I was completely shocked by how many parents had been in a similar situation with their kids and complete strangers. A former student (from my first year of teaching high school) was chided for allowing her son to play with her tablet device while they waited in line to check out. The stranger called the kid spoiled and told the parent that they were ruining him by allowing him all these fancy toys. Others reported unsolicited advice during their child's raging meltdown from strangers at the grocery. Some even had their children ridiculed for their dress, their hair, and what kind of shoes they wore.

Was I harsh on the old bag in my letter?

Probably.

Did I send it?

No.

Did it make me feel a little better at the end of a grueling day of parenting?

Yes. Mission accomplished.

Back to Missin My Kids

Comments such as "Juzt got out of jail" send a big, red flag, but the comments that she made regarding wanting to write him tell me that there is some remorse and that she would like to try to make good. She lost her rights to Eli, but that doesn't mean she can't keep in touch from a distance. Right now, that seems like a good idea. So why do I document this? For one, it's a record for us and eventually for Eli. It will be hard for him to accept and understand that he was taken away from these two when he was young, but having this account may help him understand why. And two, for those haters out there that think gays shouldn't be parents, we offer up this healthy dose of insanity as proof otherwise. Here are some more direct cut and pastes from her page, no edits, except for my comments, have been made.

Dramatis Personae: Eli's mom is A and his dad is L.

BOUTS TO GO TO THE DOCTORS! FEEL LIKE SHYT! GOT UP PUKING THIS MORNING! UGH! IS THERE ANY SUCH THING AS A GOOD MAN? CUZ ALL THE ONES I KNO IS ALL THE SAME!

Will There Ever Be A Man That Loves Me For Me?!? Ha, I Doubt It! Why Must Men Be Stupid And Play Games?!? L is Gone, I Love Him But We Wont Be Together Ever Again, Ill Write Him And Be Here For Him But Thats About It! UGH...I Hate Men!

Broke A PPO Order His Mom Had On Him, he's in jail

So L Is In Jail! Juss Fucking Lovely! Ugh...I Hate Men! He Will Do 90 Days Then Be Free Again! Well I Cant Go See Him! But I Will Write Him! ILY Babe ♥!

Wow...Come To Find Out L Has 3 Kids On The Way! How Ironic Is That! And He Still Loves them And A Whole Lot Of Other Chicks! Does He Even Kno What Love Is?!? Apperantly Not!! So He Can Go Be With One Of Them, Oh Wait, Thats Rite He's With her Rite Now, Cuz She Got Money! Men Are Dicks!!

Ugh Cant sleep! This Shit Sux! I Know He's Been Wit A For The Last 2 Days! Im Not Stupid! Life Sux! Dont Even Wanna Be Alive! Who Wants To Get Drunk?!? I DO I Do! Hmmm Not A Bad Idea!!

And once, I found this, a rare moment of clarity from A:

bored! Need domething to do! been sick and in bed all day! god im never getting pregnant again! Have youh ever sat bacc and looked at your life and actually think about how many people have been there? if not i highly recommend it! and the outcome will surprise youh too see how many people arent there anymore!

But then it goes back to this:

Yes, I Have A High Class, A Ghetto Ass, Luscious Thighs, Candy Eyes, Tempting Lips, Killah Kiss, So Wave Good-Bye && Blow A Kiss Cuz Baby Youh Cant Handle This

And back to stuff like this:

*The Only People I Need In My Life Are My Girls, Minus 3 Other People, That Cant Be In My Life, But I SOO WISH THEY WERE, Mommy Loves Youh Guys.! *I WILL SEE THEM ALL AGAIN ONE DAY* Even If I HafTa Wait Til They Turn 18!!* (I am assuming that she is talking about the kids that were taken away from her, including Eli)

But the icing on this freak cake was this rather unsavory turn of events:

September of 2011 was an insane month, and our lives were not our own. Between work, school commitments, and football, we were crazy busy. But that week, something happened that I can honestly say stopped my heart and probably took ten years off my life. I was at home that afternoon, and my cell phone rang. It was Eli's social worker. Her voice, normally bouncy and light, was sullen and decidedly dark. She was very matter-of-fact as she shared with me that Eli's birth father had contacted her to let her know that both he and Eli's birth mother were HIV positive. They didn't know when they contracted it, but they were now, at this time, positive. I stood in our kitchen in stunned silence as I let her talk for a bit more (what she said, I don't know or remember), and the wheels of terror started turning in my head. I know a lot about HIV and how it's spread and contracted. But most of that is from a gay perspective. I have never had to deal with HIV from a straight perspective.

I thanked the social worker for her call, and she choked up a bit as she said "Tom, I am so sorry. Please let me know what you find out." I called our family physician and had a pretty frank conversation with the woman who answered the phone. She gave me a whole host of ideas for what to do. We decided that it would be best for the local hospital to do the lab work, so I had her send over a standing order. In the meantime, I called Tod at work and shared the information. He had a meeting after work, but he said that he would skip the meeting to come and get Eli to take him to get the blood drawn. I can't tell you what was going on in his head, but he was calm and collected. I love him for that. He is my rock when shit like this goes down. We had a brief chat, as he was in his classroom with his students, and we both went on with our days.

Tod Chimes In: *I will admit I am terrible at letting my classroom phone go to voice mail. I was mid-sentence when the phone rang, told my students to hold that thought and answered the phone. When Tom dropped the bomb on me, I was standing in front of a full classroom of sixth graders. I couldn't really ask him questions or vocalize what was running though my head. I hung up, internally freaking out, and finished the lesson. It was a good thing I had been teaching the same subject for the past 22 years and could teach the lesson without thinking. I called him back the second the students were out of the room.*

I never expected this to happen this way. After dodging the HIV bullet for three decades, I thought for sure that it would be me that would be positive and not my adopted son. One summer, a fellow dad and I were sitting on Oval Beach watching the multitude of kids frolic in front of us on the shores of Lake Michigan. There were bunches of them, from all walks of life. There were many that were physically handicapped, a few that had mental or emotional handicaps, many from other countries, and there were some that honestly defied description. We began a conversation that some will consider insensitive, but bear with me on this. He made the comment that we as LGBT parents are often the ones that come in and pick up the trash left by the heterosexual birthparents. That was tough to hear as I would never consider a child trash. However, many of these kids were tossed aside when life got too tough, or when the kids became an inconvenience, or when the law had to step in and take over. Some were deemed "unadoptable" because of their illnesses or conditions, yet here they were thriving in their new homes.

Eli was one of those kids. It hurts to check out Eli's birth parents' erratic Facebook pages as they both have pictures of him and list him as their child. Yes, you created this child, but you also abused and neglected him. You may have had the plumbing to make this work, but you didn't have the mindset, the capacity, or sobriety to raise a child in a loving home. In the time since Eli's birth and removal from their custody, his birth parents have had several more children with a variety of other parents. Eli's family tree is fodder for the Maury Show.

Because of the timing of when we had the lab work done and the time it takes to process, we spent five days in a fugue state of sorts. I went to work on Thursday after a fitful night of sleep and told my Dean the situation. I needed someone besides Tod and the social worker to know our situation. He was understanding and told me to do what I needed to do. Thursdays are my long day at the college. I am there for about 13 hours. I did what I could to stay focused, but my thoughts continually turned to Eli and the news we got from Amy. I spent some time looking up information on HIV and pregnancy, and there was a glimmer of hope as I learned that most kids born from women who are HIV positive usually are okay if they are not breastfed and care is taken during the birth to protect them from further infection. I seriously doubt that Eli's mom breastfed him as that would have totally interfered with her drinking and drug use. I checked out a recent wall post on her Facebook page, and she alluded to the fact that she couldn't wait for this (pregnancy) to be over so she could get stoned again and resume her partying ways.

As we waited for Eli's test results to come back that weekend, we spent some time getting the house ready for winter. I always have this day in October or November floating around in my head each spring as I drag out all the stuff for our lives outside during the spring/summer months. I know that we'll have to get a sitter to watch the kids while we put all that stuff away in the fall, which is what we did this past weekend. Eli napped, and Anna played with the sitter while we busied ourselves, barely talking about the situation as we loaded up the cars for recycling and the Goodwill store. I spent the majority of the weekend mentally kicking myself for not being more patient with Eli and replayed scenarios in my head when his toddler behavior got the best of me. I felt like a monster, thinking about this kid and all the times that I yelled at him or have been less than tolerant of his antics as a three-year-old.

A happy time with my little man.

We made it through the weekend and had a good time with the two kids. Tempers were short and emotions were running on 11 because Sunday naps never happened for the kids or us. At one point, Tod and I talked about the situation, and we stepped into the "what if?" zone, a dangerous place to be with something like this. We had not told our parents or Eli's foster parents, so we made a mental list of who we would tell and discussed the ramifications. It was not a good conversation, but it was one we needed to have just in case. At any public school or childcare institution, all kids are treated as potential bio-hazards. Any parent will agree that kids can be a hazard. Between the nose picking, the booger eating and the poor potty hygiene, it's a wonder they live to see five. They are walking petri dishes with grabby hands and runny noses. This was different, but we knew that he would be treated fairly and with respect when he got to school. The ignorance and fear that permeated the early years of this disease are long gone.

It was unseasonably warm that weekend, and I made the mistake of drinking a glass of iced tea on Sunday afternoon. My sleep on Sunday night was less than restful. We went about our business Monday morning, and when I arrived at the college, I called the doctor's office to see if the test results were available. The woman who answered the phone told me that the test came back negative and that Eli was okay. I started crying on the phone as I thanked her and asked her what we needed to do next. The doctor was right there, and he said we were okay, Eli was safe. My hands were shaking as I called Tod and shared the good news.

So now what? Eli is fine and healthy, but his birth family is sick. We have asked Eli's social worker to keep us posted and to let us know what is up with their situation. I shared this with our daycare provider; she grabbed me, hugged me and asked why we didn't tell her so she could have shared in our stressful weekend as we waited for the results. I told her that sometimes you have to face things alone, deal with them as a family, and then share with the rest of the world. Tod and I shared this horrible weekend together, and it's a weekend I hope we never have to live through again.

Field Observation:
I Tinkle on Your Grave (April 2009)

If anyone knows how to get in touch with that midget medium from *Poltergeist*, please have her call me (update: she is dead). Why, you ask? Well, I think we might have angered the dead in a big way the other night on our walk home from dinner. We went to Ted's Firehouse Pub (which is up the street from us) for their gut-busting dollar night and sucked in some greasy goodness and cheap beer. Tod had a massage, so Anna and I decided to take advantage of the great weather and walk the short walk home after dinner. Our street is a pretty diverse street. Greenwood Avenue is capped on each end with a church and houses the city's Mosque and a Hispanic church in between. There are abandoned homes as well as stately homes from the past (such as ours, natch). There is also Mount Evergreen Cemetery, the final resting place for many of Jackson's earliest residents. Some of the monuments are buffed smooth by the many years of Michigan weather. Some are amazingly ornate others are simple stones propped up in the ground. The cemetery is truly a mini mountain (hence the name), and its monument-dotted grounds roll and pitch behind wrought iron fences. As we merrily walked along Greenwood, we came across one of the few access gates along the street. Anna bolted into the cemetery and ran for a few dozen yards. I chased after her, and she finally stopped and turned back to me and said, "Papa, what is this?" as she pointed to a grave marker carved to look like a tree stump. I began telling her about how this was a place where people went after they died. Death is a relatively new concept for her thanks to a recent visit to Grandma and Grandpa McMillen. Not sure how or why the concept of death came up, but she was suddenly worried that Yukon wouldn't be around much longer when she came home. We had a nice little toddler talk, and I think she's okay with the general concept of death. Thanks Grandma!

She seemed generally interested in the headstones and deftly meandered through the cemetery. We climbed up a rather big hill and when we got to the top Anna turned to me and in her *thishastohappenrightnow* voice said, "Papa, I have to go potty!"

The cemetery one creepy morning.

Shit.

It wasn't number two; she only had to pee. We found a rather large monument for privacy, and I sized it up to guesstimate where the dearly departed may be and aimed Anna's bottom away from that spot. I don't know why I was worried about privacy in a graveyard as we were the only people roaming around that night at 7:15. Anna did her business, and I checked out the names on the monument. I said "Sorry about this" out loud and mentioned their names. Anna didn't seem to be too concerned about the wrath of the pissed on and pissed off dead and ran off to check out another large headstone.

I, however, patted the stone and reminded them that they were kids once too, and she meant no harm.

CHAPTER TWENTY-SIX:
A LOOK BACK TO ELI'S FIRST MONTHS

THE ROUTINE WAS GOOD at first, but as 4:00 pm approached each day, a sense of dread comes over me. While I am eager to see and play with my kids and husband, the other life duties get in the way. The time between 4 and 7 pm is insane as we try to balance what has to be done with what we think *should* be done. I have become good at whipping up quick and easy dinners and have done well getting food on the table in a timely manner. But, since we're trying to eat healthy, the dinner prep involves more than peeling away a plastic film to reveal the brownie. It takes time and someone has to watch the kids. The nights when Tod is at a meeting are insane. Between the cat hollering for her dinner, and the two eager kids demanding snacks, I feel more like I am on K.P. than a parent. I have found that Sponge Bob and the high chair can help facilitate dinner prep, but it's not the best parenting, and I know that. My coworkers gave Eli and Anna a great art center as a gift, and we set it up in the dining room where Anna is content to tear through and color everything she can get her hands on. Eli however, is a creature of habit, like the cat. When his hunger alarm goes off, food better be presented before him or ELSE! I have found that by breaking up a snack bar, or handing him one animal cracker at a time keeps him occupied and quiet. I hate to placate a kid with food, but this buys me time and helps with the meal prep.

So finally dinner is made, and we start to eat. I have stopped making three different meals and have begun incorporating bits and pieces of our dinner into what the kids are eating. Sounds good in theory, but it's truly amazing how far a 16-month-old can fling a plate of green beans that have suddenly become boring to him. He's more adventurous than Anna at this point and will at least try something. I once put a tablespoon of gravy on her chicken (at her request) and it turned into a 30 minute ordeal to get the gravy off the chicken. I am resisting turning dinner time into short order cooking time as I know families who have kids who will only eat this or that and the parents end up cooking separate meals for all involved. A friend of ours has a grandchild that only eats chicken nuggets and little else. I know a bit about the young child's dietary needs, and according to our physician, they will not starve to death if they pick and peck at their food.

But back to the table and dinner; we used to be able to start with a prayer, but once Eli sees the food, it's over and his caveman grunts and howls become pretty loud while we offer a brief thanks. I added to this blessing to our prayer at tonight's meal as Eli wailed in protest of this spiritual delay: "… and God bless Eli as he is apparently starving to death." It was greeted with a grunt and a fist on the table. He must have some Viking in him. I have accepted the fact that those halcyon days of yore when we would listen to music and talk about adult subjects and not have to referee food fights are over for the time being.

After dinner, the bed time rituals start. Eli goes down first and is a dream, so we are lucky with that. He's out by 7pm and sleeps through until we go and rouse him in the morning. Anna, however, requires a committee and a UN Peace Keeping Force to get her into the bedroom. She is the queen of negotiation and will twist your words and your patience as she resists settling in for the night. I don't know what her problem is. She knows when she is tired ("Papa, you know I only pick my nose when I am tired…" as she stands there in front of you picking her nose), and she understands that she feels better after a nap or a good night's sleep. Plus, she has, in my opinion, a rockin' room. There are books and tons of toys, plus a really cool bed. I'd be in heaven if someone told me to go there and stay put. Most nights she goes right to bed, but some nights are filled with banging on the door and the pathetic whines of:

"I'm thiiiiiiiiiiiiiiiirsty"

"I'm hunnnnnnnnnnnnngry"

Then there are the brain-jolting screams at 3 am for no apparent reason. I guess we are paying the price for having her sleep through the night at an early age.

I remember seeing an article in *Parents* Magazine about how parents can make time for themselves, and in typical *Parents* Magazine style, they presented a bucolic view of these two parents' evening routine. The highly posed and stylized photo had the tag line: *It's 10 pm and the kids are in bed, so Marcia works on updating their children's scrapbooks while John checks the latest sports scores and stock reports."*

BULL SHIT!

If it is 10 pm here, my ass is in or near bed and the only thing I am working on updating is my beer consumption. Seriously, as Barney Frank so eloquently asked, "on what planet do you spend most of your time?" By the time the kids are in bed, the kitchen is cleaned, and we have prepped for the next day, it's usually around 8 or 9pm. Then our other work begins, emails checked, blogs read or written and the occasional DVR'd program to watch.

Scrapbooking?

Maybe Eli and Anna will get one when they are in high school. Were it not for one of Tod's coworkers creating a baby book for Anna, we'd have no physical record of her first year. So yeah, the hobbies are out for now. I have learned to watch and enjoy *Top Chef* on fast forward and have begun to skip the interviews on the *Daily Show*. Our Netflix selections sit patiently on top of the TV in hopes that one day we'll watch them. I recall my mom talking about watching this movie of the week or this special on ABC when I was a kid. Much hype and discussion occurred and when the big night finally came, it would be Doug, my dad, and I watching while my mom slept sitting up on the couch. I now know how she feels.

There are some nights when Tod and I barely speak to each other before we collapse in bed. But then the alarm goes off the next morning, and the day begins again.

Once Eli is up and around, Anna will call out from her room to be "waked up" by Eli. She loves to have him come in and pounce on her bed. The squeals that drive me crazy at dinner time are fun and endearing at the 6 a.m. hour as her little brother beats on the bed to find his big sister.

And then the day begins again.

Breakfasts are made, lunches packed, and Nickelodeon watched. Would I trade this for anything else? Hell no. These two are the best things (after Tod) that have ever happened to me.

Chapter Thirty-Seven: Things I Have Learned Since Becoming a Parent

Things that I have learned since becoming a parent:

- *iCarly* is pretty damn funny. No, really, it is. Her brother Spencer is a riot and her BFF Sam is a mini-version of Sam on *Sex in the City*. Honestly, how many 'tweens actually say: "Momma likes the meat!" Oh, and Carly's love interest Freddie is damn cute. And before you call Chris Hansen, he's 20. Relax.
- *Imagination Movers*: Two of them are hot and make our morning breakfast TV much more interesting. I will let you Google them and make your own decisions.
- Snow White is indeed the fairest of them all. You other Disney Princesses better step down NOW.
- Kids' bandages are the bomb. I love going to work with Handy Manny on my own boo boos. Added bonus, they actually stick.
- Time is not your own. This is a shocker. The good thing is people understand when you have kids between 2 and 5 and cut you slack. Not sure how this will play when they are older. I am milking it for all it's worth now.
- The Wiggles are annoying. Thankfully, Anna only requested them once and we moved on.
- Kids' hair products reek of rotten fruit and or Jolly Ranchers left in your car in the summer. No one wants to smell rotten green apples first thing in the morning. Ever.
- I can't imagine a life without wipes at my beck and call at this point. Seriously, I think we have a pack in every room in our house. Not to mention our cars.

- Library fines, they tend to go up as the kids spread their books far and wide after bringing them home from the library.

Hipster kid, hipster dad.

What have YOU learned?

I posed this question to my Facebook peeps for consideration. Here is what came in:

- THAT EVERYTHING MY PARENTS TOLD ME, TAUGHT ME. WHICH I RESISTED SO MUCH...TURNED OUT TO BE TRUE
- I truly learned what unconditional love is...and am now able to share it with my partner.
- How unbelievably fierce love can be. Now I understand what my mom meant when she said I would always be her "baby."
- However annoying I thought our mobile song was, I LOVE the tune now that it keeps baby girl smiling for a half hour. In fact, I even hum it around the house now...
- I learned to celebrate every day and make life an amazing, passionate journey!!
- I really can function on six hours of sleep!

- I learned that having a Tonka-tough daredevil of a little girl is way more fun than having the little boy I *thought* I wanted :) Oh, and *Yo Gabba Gabba* is pretty awesome, too.
- My son renewed my love of cartoons, and my daughter led me to *Yo Gabba Gabba*.
- That you can blame any of your embarrassing shows on "I watch it for the kids, they like it.
- Thanks to *Ni Hao Kai-Lan*, I can now say "thank you" and "grandfather" in Chinese! Who says children's programing isn't educational...
- I read somewhere that parenthood is the same stress level as starting a new job every day. You are always learning and never know what to expect!
- It's so not about me anymore
- That quiet children are naughty
- *Sesame Street* is the best show on TV and quiet usually means trouble and a big mess to clean up.
- Have to leave the bathroom door open a bit so you can hear what they're up to.
- That the capacity with which I loved prior to my children coming into my life was shockingly shallow. They have given me a depth to my feelings that I didn't know existed.

I was sharing all this with a fellow parent in one of my pottery classes, and we were discussing how much time we spend with our kids each day. She is currently on sabbatical from her job and realized how much time work takes away from time together with her family. When I sat down and figured out our schedule and how much time we actually spend with the kids, it saddened me deeply. We are up at 6:30, and we all eat breakfast together. Tod and Eli are out the door at 7:45 or so, and Anna and I hang out and wait for her bus which usually comes around 8:05.

Let Apple babysit your kids.

Time together: 90 minutes

Eli is picked up after his nap at daycare around 4, and Anna gets home on the bus around 4:15. We will usually do something special, like a trip to the library, or a trip to the park, or we'll relax in the attic family room, depending on our mood. Dinner is at 6, and the kids are usually in bed by 7 or 7:30.

Time together: 3 hours, 45 minutes

Week day total: around 5 hours.

We suck.

I am not sure what the remedy is at this point, aside from one of us quitting our job and homeschooling our kids. This observation bothered me, but in our modern times, I guess this is what we have to do. Make every moment count and love them when you can, even if they are driving you nuts.

Field Observation:
Daddy/Papa Daughter Dance (February 2010)

When we walked into the Jackson Parks and Rec's Annual Daddy/Daughter Dance this weekend, Beyoncé's *Single Ladies* was thumping from the speakers on the dance floor. I had to giggle as I peered into the darkened convention center and saw a teeming mass of cuteness bobbing up and down to this tiresome song. Oh sure, it was fun the first time you heard it, and the first 4,000 tribute dance videos were fun too. But to see this much unbridled glee was energizing and brought new life to the song. I questioned the appropriateness of this song for a dance aimed at 3 to 16-year-olds, but I quickly reminded myself *not* to be one of those dads. We got in line and had our picture taken, after all, we did look pretty spiffy. We then headed into the noise and began looking for Anna's BFF Chloe (who, it turns out, didn't get a ticket in time). Instead we found a friend from school and all was good. We danced, we ran around, we lost Anna for a brief and terrifying moment, and we wished we would have brought earplugs. Honestly Miley Cyrus sucks at any level, but when cranked up to 11, the suck hurts.

The past few weeks had been rough at home as the crud that was going around had been lingering at our house longer than I expected. One got better, another got sick. We were tired, we were sick; we were not feeling all the best, and that can make things tense and crazy. However, this night, with Eli at home with the grandparents, we were able to go out and have a good time together. As we moved around the hall dancing and bobbing along to the music, I saw many different daddies and daughters, some were older, and some were younger. Some were all spiffed up; others apparently rolled out of bed and came as they were. But I also saw a young girl of about 15 in a red carpet worthy gown, her hair done up in a perfect glamour girl 'do topped with a lovely tiara. Her older father followed behind this young diva with a smile that said "I am so proud of my daughter right now I could burst!" Never mind the fact that the girl had Down syndrome, she was rockin' the look and was takin' names with her fabulousness. I had to turn away as I saw a young dad holding his daughter as they danced. The chemotherapy was obviously taking its toll on this girl's body as she was a little, bald, bag of bones in her lovely dress and father's arms. She looked so happy and glad to be there, it made a lump rise up in my throat as I thought about what must have been going through her dad's mind. I said a quick prayer of thanks that my girl was healthy and well and chided myself for all the times I yelled at her. There was also a dad with the back of his shaved head tattooed with a flaming skull. From the front, he and his 13-year-old or so daughter looked like any other daddy/ daughter combo in the room. They hung back against the wall, and danced to that Miley *Party in the USA* song with abandon when it came on for the fifth time that night.

Love is unconditional, and love is something we often forget to express to those around us.

As we drove to the restaurant downtown for after dance drinks and to show off our outfits, Anna burst out an "I LOVE YOU GUYS!" from the backseat of the car. I had to steady my hands on the wheel as I stole a look at my little girl all decked out in her pink Sunday-go-to-church coat, a similar shade to the pink in the dragon suit that vexed us the other night. Parenting isn't easy, but loving your kids is.

Chapter Twenty-Eight:
And Then What Happened?
Part Two

Life with two kids under the age of ten is crazy; anyone who has been there will tell you that. The days of lingering over a page of text from the manuscript are gone. I am now lucky if I can get one page out a week. It was suggested that I tweet the rest of the book, as 140 letters is all I am able to write each day. Work, housekeeping, the never ending laundry, and the kids' insane schedule have all worked against finishing this book before the kids are out of high school. It has now been three years since Eli came to live with us and life is good. Busy, but good. The drama of the first summer has been replaced by day to day drama that only an older sister and younger brother can bring to a household. We have been told to sit back and let them figure their own problems out. But we have also noticed that when we do that, we are precariously close to having to call 911. Eli is now portable and is out of diapers and the big car seat. He started preschool this year, and he loves it. He's my daily companion in the car as his school is located on the campus where I teach. It is funny to watch him develop after watching his sister tear through the developmental milestones in a heartbeat. Eli is on Eli time, and that's okay. At one point, we were worried about his speech development, but now as he is in an educational setting each day, his speech, diction, and ability to communicate grows with leaps and bounds. With his social history, specifically the bad choices his birth-parents made both before and after he was born, gave us reason to be concerned. But he is fine. He's a boy. Anna blazed the trail for us as new parents, and Eli meanders down that path at his own speed.

We have been asked if we are going to do the second-parent adoption (for me) with Eli, and at this time, we have not. The judge that did Anna's adoption is no longer doing them for people that do not live in his jurisdiction. We decided that we could not move from our home nor could we take on any more debt to make this happen. We have the necessary paperwork filed to ensure that I am his guardian, but beyond that, legally I am nothing to Eli.

He may call me Papa, but that's it.

Because of Tod's adoption of both kids, Eli and Anna are legally siblings. Tod and I are legally married in some states, and Anna is legally my child, so where does that leave us as a family? Good question. Here in Michigan, we are two single men living together with two kids who may or may not be related to each other. Love may have made the family, but the laws of our state are working against us to keep us a family. The things that we have to worry as a non-traditional family are things that heterosexual couples never have to think about. If anything were to happen to Tod, it is unclear what would happen with Eli and my ability to continue raising him as my child. I shudder at that thought but also say "BRING IT!" We'd be an ideal test case to see if the Defense of Marriage Act is indeed enforceable in our situation that involves two states and two separate laws regarding marriage. We have faith in the government (perhaps foolishly so) that one day we will be a legal family in our home state of Michigan and that horrible thoughts such as these will never be thought of again.

Chapter-Nine:
Ancora Imparo

Since my Renaissance Art History class back in my college years, I have loved the work and ideals of Michelangelo. When my professor started showing us slides of his work in the museum's lecture hall my heart leapt and my imagination soared. The majesty of the Sistine Chapel is incomprehensible at times. Someday I hope to see it in person with my own two eyes instead of pictures in a book or on the web. This three-decade love-affair has included reading everything I can on the Master, and it was while I was reading a book on him that I discovered his alleged last words: *Ancora Imparo*, or, "Still, I learn." Great words from a great man, although, I believe my last words would probably be: "Fire this doctor NOW!" I decided before we had kids that I wanted those words tattooed on me some day, so I began playing with the words and the fonts. I printed it out a million different ways and taped them onto every conceivable place on my person. I thought it was a pretty nifty tattoo idea, as I had never seen it before. We were in Chicago a few months later and Tod came up to me at a garden center and took me over to see the tattoo of the girl behind the counter. She had a sleeveless top on and coming out from the straps on the back of the garment were what I thought were MY words.

DAMNIT Chi-town Hipster Chick, you beat me to it!

After I calmed down and my desire to kill subsided, I started looking at how she presented her tattoo and realized that we had two completely different concepts of how to ink this on ourselves. After talking to her, I found out that she was a design major (natch) and was in love with the Vivaldi font and its flowing lines. I didn't care so much about the font as I did the meaning behind the words, so I soldiered on with my idea, but tabled it for a few years.

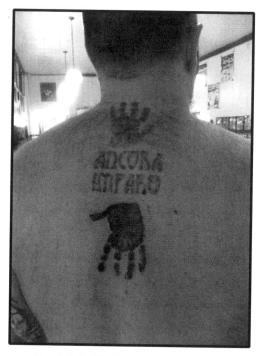

Fresh ink. No, I am not a Wookie.

Flash forward to 2005, and we are new dads and the new little one in my life was presenting me with challenges each and every day. As we went through with Tod's adoption of Anna, he got her footprints turned into a stylized heart on his chest with her name above it. I decided that since I was an artist and used my hands for a living, I would go with her hand print. So one night we inked her up and the two of us struggled to get her ink-covered mitt onto a piece of paper in my sketchbook. I wish we would have filmed it as it was pretty funny. I worked with our amazing tattoo guy, and we centered the hand above the words of Michelangelo, a fitting touch to my new role as parent. It was tattooed at the base of my neck (see above). Depending on what kind of shirt I am wearing, the tattoo is pretty much invisible except for the tips of Anna's hand poking out above the collar line. Five years later, I added Eli's hand print below the words, pointing down my back. His hand is much larger than Anna's 10 month old hand, but it will be a marker for how old he was when he came to live with us.

Jesus Has Two Daddies

Each day does present its challenges, and each day I continue to learn and grow with my family. This is something I hope to do until the day I die.

ACKNOWLEDGEMENTS:

I may be listed as the author of this book, but there were many people who assisted me along the way. I'd like to take a moment and thank them here.

First off, my loving husband Tod. Without him and his unwavering love and support, this book wouldn't be possible. Thank you Tod for all you do.

Thanks to the amazing Dan Savage and Terry Hecker; without their encouragement to go forward with our story, this book would have never been written. I am appreciative of their time and insight into the world of books that warm day on Oval Beach in Saugatuck, MI. Their It gets better project is an inspiration to us all. More here: http://www.itgetsbetter.org/

It's a very ancient saying, but a true and honest thought, that if you become a teacher, by your pupils you'll be taught.

With that said, many thanks to Katie Phelan for her amazing insight into editing and story structure. Without her, my awareness of comma splices would be non-existent.

The title of this book came from a lovely children's sermon given by Pastor Beatrice Robinson the first Sunday we returned home with Anna. Her words to the children of the church were graceful, inspiring, and a fierce way to introduce our daughter to the congregation.

Thanks to Michael Miller, editor of the Toledo Free Press for letting me share his story. You can read Miller's entire article here: http://www.toledofreepress.com/2010/04/23/mercury-rising/

A special thanks to the fine people of 2 Moon Press for their support and insight.

And lastly, thanks to Anna's mom and her family. Without you and your faith in our ability to raise your daughter, this story would not have been possible. Much love from us all.